17·33

D1760312

GET YOUR
BLACK BELT
IN MARKETING

81 Power Moves
to Outperform, Outmaneuver,
and Outsmart the Competition

Master
ALI PERVEZ

Morgan James Publishing • New York

GET YOUR BLACK BELT IN MARKETING

by Ali Pervez © 2009 all rights reserved.

Library of Congress Control Number: 2008934123
ISBN: 978-1-60037-482-1   (Paperback)
ISBN: 978-1-60037-483-8   (Hardcover)

Published by:
Morgan James Publishing
1225 Franklin Avenue Suite 325
Garden City, NY 11530-1693

Toll Free 800-485-4943
www.MorganJamesPublishing.com

Cover & Interior Design by:
3 Dog Design
www.3dogdesign.net

General Editor:
Heather Campbell

Habitat
for Humanity®
Peninsula
Building Partner

In an effort to support local communities, raise awareness and funds, Morgan James Publishing donates one percent of all book sales for the life of each book to Habitat for Humanity.

Get involved today,
visit www.HelpHabitatForHumanity.org.

DEDICATION

To my mother, Anees. I love you.

CONTENTS

THE BLACK BELT MARKETING
CREDOS

"I will never abuse or misuse the power of marketing. It will always be used for the benefit and good of mankind."

"I will have others' interests ahead of my own interests at all times. I am here to serve others."

"I will use the power that black belt marketing gives me to bring to market products and services that I know will make a positive difference in the lives of others."

"I will defend products and services that can add positive value to the lives of others. I understand they cannot talk; I am their voice."

"I will uphold to the highest ethical standards of marketing and make a positive contribution to the field of marketing."

"I know marketing brings good things to life. It is what makes the invisible visible and the visible valuable. I am grateful to have the power to make this happen."

"I am grateful to all the marketing masters—past, present, and future— for making this world a better place."

"Problems cannot be solved by the same level of thinking that created them."

Albert Einstein

ACKNOWLEDGEMENTS

I would like to thank a few key people who have been instrumental in bringing this book to reality. First, thanks to my wife, Ayesha, who allowed me to dedicate precious family time to the research and writing of this book, and for her ongoing love and support. Thank you! Without your support, this book would not be here today.

Next, I would like to thank Beth Bednar, who has seen my marketing career develop over the years. Thank you so much for being a dear friend, and for your confidence in my abilities. Thank you for editing this book. You took it a few notches up from the original manuscript!

Special thanks to Margo Toulouse at Morgan James Publishing for all your help. You are one of the best account representatives that I have ever worked with.

I would also like to acknowledge Publication Services, Inc., as the editorial service that makes this book read like a best seller; you did an amazing job at "sharpening the sword."

I would also like to thank my friends Stu Matlow and Ed Aitken for assisting in editing the book. I tremendously respect you both.

Thank you, John Shaw and Tom Hansen. You sent me on my career many years ago and are probably the nicest guys I have ever met. I really value our friendship.

Special thanks also go to one of my mentors and extended family member David Hancock, founder of Morgan James Publishing. Your energy is contagious! Thank you for all of your support.

Thanks also to the great marketing mentors I have had over the years for teaching me all that I know today and for generously sharing your wisdom, insight, knowledge, and talent. You are remarkable individuals, who have made me who I am. This includes Bill Jones, Bill Biedenharn, Holly Hartz, Teresa Adkins, John Spence, and David Chiang. Thank you for your patience in teaching me!

I am grateful to Matt Clark for his support during the time I was writing this book. You are well on your way to being a true black belt marketer.

Finally, thanks to Zayed Khan. Thanks for always keeping me in your prayers. You are like my brother.

Most of all, thank you, the reader, for purchasing this book. I hope it not only meets your expectations but also far exceeds them. Enjoy!

INTRODUCTION

When the student is ready, the master will appear. Now it's your turn to earn your black belt in marketing. All it takes is eighty-one moves!

The mere fact that you are reading this book tells me a lot about you. You are most probably in the top 1 percent of business people in the world, because you have figured out the connection between sales and marketing: marketing is no more than a tool used to generate sales. Congratulations, you have passed your first test in earning your black belt in marketing!

I would like to thank you for giving me the opportunity to be your teacher. You won't be disappointed. I intend to give back far more than you could ever expect from me. I am a black belt marketer, and one of my credos is that I can only become successful when you are successful. I am here to ensure your success.

What is black belt marketing?

In martial arts, a black belt is a high honor and the ultimate in self-defense. As a black belt marketer, you will know and work with proven revenue-generating strategies. Using the techniques in this book will almost certainly generate significant revenue for your organization. Black belt marketing professionals are highly trained in the most powerful and cutting-edge marketing tools available and know how to get maximum results with minimal effort. The magic word black belt marketing professionals use is leverage, or the ability to get a lot from a little. Highly trained martial arts black belts can drop a person to the floor in two moves. In the same way, black belt marketers are not people you want to compete with, because they have immense marketing muscle and know how to handle the competition. In fact, there usually is no competition. Mastering just a few of the moves in this book will change the way you market forever.

In life we don't become successful by working hard, we become successful by making the right moves. In this book, you will learn eighty-one powerful marketing moves. Why eighty-one moves? Because it takes eighty-one moves to earn a first-degree Tae Kwon Do black belt. Coincidentally, when I studied the most powerful moves to generate sales revenue, I also came up with eighty-one moves.

Through history, marketing has gone through three main phases:

PHASE 1: OLD-SCHOOL MARKETING
How to write advertisements that sell and how to broadcast those messages to as many people as possible. "Get the message out."

PHASE 2: MODERN-DAY MARKETING
How to get through to busy people and make them buy in the shortest possible time.

PHASE 3: BLACK BELT MARKETING
Helping and serving others to the highest degree possible. Solving their problems and knowing that their success is your success. Providing maximum value in the shortest period of time. Building long-term, and lasting, relationships.

Black belt marketers use the tools of marketing to bring value to the marketplace. They are experts in seeing and seizing opportunities faster than others do.

Most business owners think that having a great product will guarantee success. But having a great product, service, or idea will get you only halfway there. The other half is convincing the market, for only then will you be able to sell it. This book will teach you the other half of the equation: How to sell your product by using the most powerful and cutting-edge marketing techniques on the planet.

You will learn simple and proven revenue-generating strategies: Strategies that have been and are currently being used by some of the world's top corporations, marketing gurus, and advertising agencies. These people understand that marketing in the business world is only a tool used to generate sales. Once you master the moves in this book, you will realize that black belt marketing is just a legal license to print money, and it's all about focus!

These marketing moves have been used for centuries and are rarely discussed in the public forum, because they are truly worth millions of dollars for those who choose to apply them.

In today's business world there is little downtime to formulate a plan on how to generate sales revenue. Yet most revenue-generating strategies have been tried, tested, and proven. During a live talk in London in 1952, the late Dr. Albert Schweitzer, the winner of the 1952 Nobel Peace Prize, was asked, "Doctor, what is the biggest challenge in our society today?" His response: "People do not think."

That was well over fifty years ago, but the same applies today. People react instead of thinking through a response. We live in a reactionary world that makes it is easier not to think than to think. That is why this book does the thinking for you. All the moves in this book have been thought out, because black belt marketers fight with their minds, not with their hands or feet. Those who succeed in business know that a little bit of intelligence can go a long way in marketing.

My passion is to empower as many people as possible to market effectively in business, personal, and social arenas. Although this book focuses on business, the concept of marketing in all arenas is the same: to bring value to others.

Each move could actually be a book in itself, and some are. Some moves are simple. Others are complex and take practice to master. It often takes years to earn a black belt in the martial arts. In the same way, it takes a lot of practice for someone to master these marketing moves. Certain moves will work better for certain types of businesses, but nearly all the moves can be applied, irrespective of business type and size. Start applying the moves, and you will see an immediate change in the way the market responds to you.

After you finish this book, you will never market the same again. Instead, you will be a black belt marketer. You'll be able to cut through the marketing noise and clutter and focus on revenue-generating strategies that actually bring in the success you deserve!

I hold the belief that you achieve great success when you concentrate your power to implement and exploit basic ideas to the maximum degree possible.

What I am about to teach you is the power of simplicity and logic. Thank you for allowing me to be your MGM: Marketing Grand Master.

Good luck! Let us now begin.

Ali Pervez
Marketing Grand Master
www.blackbeltinmarketing.com

MOVE

1

Understand marketing and know its purpose

MOVE 1

Understand marketing and know its purpose

To be a true black belt marketer, you will need to adopt a new way of thinking that is different from conventional marketers. You will often do the opposite of what other marketers do. You will need to develop a new mind-set, or way of thinking, about marketing. In the world of black belt marketing, mind-set is always more important than method. The techniques will follow naturally once you adopt the mind-set. So let's get started by asking the obvious question: What is marketing?

Marketing is the process of bringing value to the market. It is value that customers—or soon-to-be customers—believe to be important that enhances their lives. Marketers call it perceived value. People buy products and services they believe can improve their lives. Knowing that marketing is about perceived value is a secret that marketing gurus have known for centuries. It is a jealously guarded secret, and now you know it, too.

True black belt marketers stay focused on the customer, not the competition. The customer or potential customer should always be at the core of your thinking.

GET YOUR BLACK BELT IN MARKETING

"There is no objective reality. There are no facts. There are no best products. All that exists in the world of marketing are perceptions in the mind of the customer. This perception is reality."

—Jack Trout and Al Ries

"Marketing is about perceived value."

—Professor Donald Sexton
Trump University/Columbia University

A black belt marketer's goal is to be "on the mark" of the perceived value that others want. It's called marketing for that reason: to be on the mark of what the market wants and values.

Mark >>>>>>> Market >>>>>> Marketing!

You will find that most of your competition focuses on how great their product or service is. They have it all backward. They are in love with their products' or services' wonderful features instead of with customers. But a black belt marketer is in love with customers first—how the product or service can add value for its customers. As a black belt marketer, you must figure out what your customers value and how to deliver that perceived value. When you do, you win the game of marketing!

The goal of the black belt marketer is not to present a product or service to soon-to-be customers but to show them how they can gain immense benefit and maximum value from an offering. Black belt marketers care for the success of their customers more than anyone else ever will. A black belt marketer never makes anyone buy anything but helps others make informed decisions.

I will now share with you another of the biggest and best-kept secrets in marketing: The best product or service does not always win; the product that enables the customer to make a decision in the shortest amount of time will win every time.

MOVE 1: UNDERSTAND MARKETING AND KNOW ITS PURPOSE

When prospects approach you, they already have identified a problem they think you can potentially solve. Your job is to convince them you can. You help people make the right choices by providing as much information as possible. Here's another way to look at it:

Product or service   =   **What solves the problem**
Marketing   =   **How it does it**

Black belt marketers are the best teachers and educators in the world! They show people how their product or service solves problems.

Top marketers know that education is the best way to market. Educate your prospects and customers on how it is in their best interest to deal with you and no one else. Unless you continually educate your market, people will not appreciate the value you can bring to them. For example, if I am trying to sell you a health supplement, simply telling you what it is will not impress you. But if I educate you on the physiological benefits that the health supplement may have on your body and how people of your age group are experiencing more energy and vibrancy using this health supplement, I now will have a greater chance of getting your attention and making a sale.

When a well-qualified prospect appears (someone with a true interest in your offer), the only thing standing between that prospect and a purchase is the education she needs to see you as the best solution. Education helps customers make informed decisions.

Never forget the end game of marketing is always to improve and make others' lives better with your product or service.

When you adopt this mind-set, failing in business in unlikely. Marketing becomes easy because you never sell but instead help others buy. People are always looking for help. Your message should focus on how your product or service brings value to customers, and, as such, they will naturally become interested in you. Once they understand you want to help

5

them, they will want to help you by buying your product or service. The mind-set is the prospect and customer first, you later.

Marketing is not about manipulation or making money. It is about serving customers at the highest level possible and showing them you can solve their problems. Money is simply the reward for doing this. In its purest form, marketing is about enhancing the quality of others' lives. If you are a medical sales representative, you are selling products that can even save lives!

Black belt marketers differ from conventional marketers, whose message is self-serving. Your approach is to serve others—to improve, enhance, and add value to their lives. Most of the competition you face on a daily basis has its own self-interest at heart. As a black belt marketer, you will put your customers' success ahead of your own. You know your customers' success is your success, and you'll do whatever it takes to make them successful.

Always aim to deliver maximum value in the shortest possible time. For example, a company may have cash flow problems and need sales in the next thirty days to cover expenses. You would recommend that they ask all their existing customers for referrals. We will cover this in move number ten. This will add maximum value in the shortest period of time. In the past, the company may have assumed that its customers will provide referrals; now it asks for them!

This way you will succeed. The world pays for value—it's the honey that bees are attracted to! Once you show your product or service is invaluable to the market, you will immediately attract the bees!

You have a moral obligation to both the product/service you represent and the market.

Product	Marketing	Market
Service		Customer
What you have		What people value

MOVE 1: UNDERSTAND MARKETING AND KNOW ITS PURPOSE

Marketing simply marries products and services with the market. You are a broker.

Now that you understand the purpose of marketing, which is to serve and bring value to others, let's move to strategies to make this happen.

MOVE
2

Make sure you've got the goods

MOVE 2

Make sure you've got the goods

Before we dive into specific black belt marketing strategies, we need to verify you've got the goods. The starting point of all successful marketing programs is a tested, robust, and proven product or service—something that can enhance the lives of your customers.

The first questions people ask when they see a new product or service are, "Will it work for me?" "Will it really do what they say?" "Will it solve my problems?" "Will it make my life better?" "Is this just another gimmick, fad, or marketing hype?" This is why you must have the goods before starting any marketing campaign. No marketing can help you unless you have a product or service that can truly enhance the lives of others.

Have you done the research? Tested the product? Shown it to as many people as possible? Have you improved your product or service based on feedback, and now feel it's "on the mark" of what the market wants? Are you ready to market? Do you have a marketing plan? In this plan, you should have formal feedback from the market. Some organizations call this a marketing requirements document, or MRD. It can simply be a one-page summary that validates your idea.

GET YOUR BLACK BELT IN MARKETING

You must be convinced that what you offer will give immense benefit, value, and performance to your customer. Before you start marketing, you need a remarkable product, which means people will make a positive remark about it. Will they say, "Thank you for bringing this to my attention"? Don't go out to market with just another product. You must have a clearly differentiated product or service (see move 9).

More than ever, people are skeptical. Many before you have over-promised and under-delivered. There are not many marketers who truly care about making a positive impact on the world.

Your marketing is like a courtroom battle. You have to prove to the world that your product or service is "innocent" and can make a difference in peoples' lives. As a black belt marketer, you must defend your product for the betterment of humankind. Remember, in the court of marketing, you are guilty until you can prove the value of your product to others!

You are going to have to fight to get through the clutter and noise and to prove you have something the market needs and values. Yes, marketing can help you succeed, but it can just as easily destroy you. If you promote a product or a service that does not deliver, it will destroy your reputation and your credibility.

Marketing does not make something right or wrong, it simply reveals it in the shortest possible time. At the end of the day, it is the product or service that sells the product or service. It has to stand on its own if it is to survive in the competitive marketplace.

Your competition thinks that a product and marketing are one, but they are two different things. The product or service is often tangible and visible. The marketing is intangible. It is the invisible force that takes the product or service into the hands of your customers.

Black belt marketers recognize marketing as a true force. Marketing, when done correctly, will make the process of obtaining a sale very easy.

MOVE 2: MAKE SURE YOU'VE GOT THE GOODS

You must under-promise and over-deliver. Surprise your customers as much as possible. Always exceed expectations by providing more value items, gifts, bonuses, and additional services than your customer expects. This will build trust, loyalty and separate you from the competition. Statistics clearly show one satisfied customer refers, on average, three new ones, and one dissatisfied customer tells eleven others. This is why you must never get seduced into making claims you cannot support.

If you have the goods, it's time to market! Let's move on.

3

Develop clients,
not customers

MOVE 3

Develop clients, not customers

I n the first move, you learned to adopt the mind-set of a black belt marketer. It is an attitude of being of service and bringing value to others. The best way to serve others is to treat them as friends and family. It means you love them and sincerely care for their well being more than anyone else's does.

You want what is best for your customers, and you want to take care of them. Most of all, you want to protect them from making the wrong decisions. You are committed to their success. You are concerned for their well-being. You care at a far deeper level than your competitors do. Once customers recognize this, they will become your clients for life!

The difference between a customer and a client is that a customer is someone who buys from you once and a client is someone with whom you have a long-term relationship. As a black belt marketer, you are in the client—not customer—generation business. Clients are people with whom you have a deep relationship. They trust you implicitly, and they buy from you and refer to you because they love and respect you.

You should be the only choice, because you provide outstanding value faster than your competition. Black belt marketing is a mind-set of wanting to improve the lives of others, and caring for their success and well-being.

For example, let's say you gave a friend a microwave as a birthday present. What would you do after two months? You'd ask him how it was working out for him. If he was having trouble, you might give him a microwave cookbook. If after another few months he still had not used it, you might ask him to give it back because it wasn't being used! Then he may protest and use it.

Do the same with your prospects and customers. Your goal is for them to gain tremendous value from your product or service; do everything in your power to make this happen. Follow-up is powerful because it changes your mind-set about marketing and about your prospects and customers. It's the moment they start to see you differently, as well.

Several years ago, my doctor asked me to take cholesterol-lowering medication, because I have a family history of high cholesterol. I refused and told him I didn't like to take drugs. He looked me in the eye and said, "If you were my brother, this is the advice I would give you." I took the medicine, and he will be my doctor for life, because I now know he cares deeply about me as a client.

I went to see *Spider-Man 3* the other day with my kids, and they loved it. I thought of my friends, who are clients of a company I consult for. I sent them tickets with a hand-written note from the company CEO that said, "You may have heard that *Spider-Man 3* is said to be the best of the series. I want you and your family to enjoy the movie!" The clients loved it! Through this simple gesture, we treated them as clients, friends, and family. A little sincerity and intentionality set my company far apart from the competition.

Black belt marketers have real relationships with their customers, which converts them to clients. If you first serve others and your product offers them benefit and value, they will be more than happy to help you in any way you want. But, remember, it is others first.

MOVE
4

Build quality relationships
as quickly as possible

MOVE 4

Build quality relationships as quickly as possible

P eople buy from people they know, like, and trust. But what is trust? Trust is simply the prediction of an expected outcome.

You purchased this book because you trusted I could teach you some powerful revenue-generating techniques. That is your expectation. If by using this book your sales increase significantly, you will trust me more and want to develop an ongoing relationship.

A relationship begins when trust has been established.

The biggest factor preventing people from buying your product or service is a lack of trust that it will deliver on its promise and work for them. They worry about whether they are making the right decision. They are both cynical and skeptical. This is why the majority of business is conducted through referrals, because a referral is the quickest way to get to trustworthy people.

Networking, referrals, and relationship building are the top three revenue-generating moves you will learn in this book. Master these moves alone, and you will run circles around your competition.

GET YOUR BLACK BELT IN MARKETING

Black belt marketers know the way to build trust is to build a relationship first. No one will buy from you unless they have an established relationship with you. The only exception is a well-established brand. The way that you build a relationship before a sale is to invest in your prospective clients, to provide them with information and education that can help, improve, and enhance their lives. Most marketers call these things "value items." Free reports are one of the best examples of value items. People want to know you before they will invest in your product or service.

In *The Power of Focus*, we are told that Warren Buffet always makes his final investment decision based on three things:

Do I like the people I am investing with?
Do I trust the people I am investing with?
Do I respect the people I am investing with?

His final decision is always based on whether he feels he will have a good relationship with the company that he is investing with.

You must build lasting relationships to grow sales. Do this by implementing move 3, treating your prospects and customers as friends and family. The ability to build relationships quickly is an innate skill all black belt marketers possess. Black belt marketers have the ability to make customers feel like the most important people in the world, because they are!

Black belt marketers also know that one quality relationship in business is worth millions of dollars. They understand that people buy from people they know and trust, so they invest much time upfront building quality relationships before asking for the sale. They earn respect and trust first. Those untrained in black belt marketing call this small talk. But small talk makes people talk big about you!

People will even pay more for inferior products or services because they have established a relationship with the salesperson. Relationship building is a skill that is at the core of black belt marketing. Unless you learn

MOVE 4: BUILD QUALITY RELATIONSHIPS AS QUICKLY AS POSSIBLE

how to build quality relationships, you cannot earn your black belt in marketing. Relationships are the foundation of black belt marketing.

How do you build relationships? Provide as much free information as possible. This could be a sample or the ability to test-drive your product or service at no cost. Extended guarantees, taking people out for lunch or dinner, sending birthday cards or newsletters, arranging special events, and providing Web casts and conference calls are all examples of activities that will build relationships and trust.

Make strangers into customers and customers into friends (clients).

It's not easy to build trust. It can take weeks, months, sometimes years. That's why you may hear salespeople say it took them two years to break into a certain account. If you started your business from scratch, you got your first customers from your own network of friends. These people already trusted you! In the same way, as your business grows, you must continue to develop the same level of trust with people you don't know, so-called prospects. These people may be interested in buying from you but don't yet trust you.

One of the biggest mistakes business owners make is trying to sell without first building trust. Trust building comes through developing quality relationships. Unless you are a household name, no one is going to buy your product with a single presentation or letter. Even household names had to spend years building their brands. Another way to look at a brand is as a sign of trust. Trust building is part of the sales cycle. Trust building takes time. It's based on your ability to deliver on your word. Black belt marketers know that if your word is no good, you are no good.

Black belt marketers use a concept called "drip marketing." This is the process of sending weekly or monthly information to prospects to earn respect and trust slowly. Newsletters are a typical example. Drip marketing is about showing incremental value to build trust in you, your product, or your service.

23

GET YOUR BLACK BELT IN MARKETING

Invest in people, and they will invest in you. Provide free articles and information. Once you master how to gain trust by building quality relationships, you will quickly outsmart competition because trust leads to accelerated decisions.

If I am a trusted friend and I tell you about a product or service I've had a good experience with, you will more than likely try it. The time needed to make your decision is cut dramatically. As your friend, I helped you make an informed decision and did the research for you!

As we discussed earlier, black belt marketers know that no one sells, they just help people to make intelligent decisions. A referral through a friend not only enables an informed decision but also leads to an accelerated decision. Trust is already built into the equation.

There are usually only three reasons people don't buy your product or service:

1. You are unable to get your message or value proposition to them.

2. They are not true prospects, people that can benefit and gain value from your product or service.

3. They don't believe you can deliver on your promise.

Guess which is the most common reason? They don't trust you can deliver on your promises.

One of the most effective ways to build trust is a strategy known to all black belt marketers: consistency. Most companies send out information once and then stop. It's similar to a marathon runner stopping just before the finish line. People do read items sent to them—if they are factual and add value. The more people are exposed to you and your products and services, the more they trust you. Consistency builds trust. It's why marketing professionals send out informational newsletters, which add incremental value each time they are sent, a concept called drip marketing. Shower them with information they can use, such as "a tip of the day." Show them how to get the most out of your product or service. Just fifty-two tips, one per week, keeps you on their radar. How many of your competitors would do that?

Continue to send out valuable information to your customers, and they will realize that you are the real thing. Once your customers recognize this, you have earned their trust.

It takes a minimum of seven impressions to get someone to take you seriously.

The goal of marketing should be to show prospects why they should trust you: because you are a leader in the field; you can add more value; you understand their problems, pain, and issues better than your competitors. This should show in your communications with them. You want them to think, "Wow, if I can learn so much information from these mailings, what would happen if I actually developed a business relationship with these people and bought their product or service?"

At that point, you can connect with others, you can relate to them, and they can relate to you. This becomes the starting point for trust or relationship building: develop staying power. It's not a matter of if these prospects will become customers, it is when. These prospects will buy when they see the value to them. They will trust you.

Any business can use this strategy to educate prospects by sending out value items:

Type of business	Example of a value item
Dry cleaning	How to prevent allergies by having clothes dry-cleaned
Car repair company	Ideas to keep your car in top-notch condition

GET YOUR BLACK BELT IN MARKETING

Restaurants	Healthy eating tips and recommendations
Financial planner	How to develop a nest egg for retirement

Customers are looking for trustworthy people. Use your black belt to show them that you are the one they should choose.

MOVE

5

Get externally focused

MOVE 5

Get externally focused

When all is said and done, business is about solving other people's problems. We all get up every day and go to work to help other people. Money is simply the reward for doing so. To solve others' problems effectively, we need to understand their pain. The more you can relate to other people's problems, the more they will love you. The magic word in sales is empathy, the ability to relate to other people's problems with compassion.

As a businessperson, you probably started a business or got into business because you have passion and understanding about a certain subject area. But people don't buy to satisfy your interests and desires. They buy because there is a shortcoming in their lives that your product or service can fill.

Play the part of the customer. Discover what your customers will likely experience when they use your product or service. You must be totally convinced that the customer experience is something that will make them want to come back and refer you to their friends. Your marketing will be ineffective unless you have satisfied customers that turn into clients that want to go out and sell for you and refer you to others. Remember what you learned in move 2. You need to have the goods, and the goods need to provide your customers with an experience that converts them into clients, and your extended sales force.

If your product or service isn't easy or fun to use, refine it. If there is a product development issue, improve on it. Maybe you simply need to update your product or service.

Continually push your product development team or vendors to the maximum to stay in line with market requirements and expectations.

Find out exactly what your customers experience when they use your product or service and what alternatives they have. Spend one day a week playing the customer. Use your own product or service, and suggest improvements to the development team or to whomever you source it from. Order competitive products or visit competitors' stores. How do they treat you as a customer? Is their product or service easier to use than yours? What do they do differently from you? Know what your competition is up to, and always know what your customer is experiencing.

When you focus on the customer, not the competition, you focus on the right thing. Know what your competitors are doing, but do not divert the attention from your customers. Many companies try to outperform their competition, but how do these companies know the competition is doing the right thing? The truth always comes from your customers (the market), not the competition. As a black belt marketer, you must know this.

The market makes the final call on the success of a product or service, so make it your goal to understand your customers.

MOVE

6

Get as much feedback
as possible!

MOVE 6

Get as much feedback as possible!

As you learned in move 1, marketing is simply the process of bringing perceived value to the marketplace. But how do you know that what you are doing is really working? How do you know it adds value? The only way to find out is through capturing feedback. Feedback is food for champions, and, in business or life, it makes you better.

Feedback is like oxygen: an organization needs a lot of it regularly to keep alive. Feedback is what the market wants and values. It tells you, in "real time," what is changing in the marketplace. It keeps you in touch with the trends and shifts in your business arena. True marketing-driven organizations always have their antennae up, listening to what customers say about them. They then incorporate the information into product design, manufacturing, and business processes. Some call it "the voice of the customer." Be receptive to what your customers tell you. It is impossible to fail if you get and implement feedback because you will move in the direction your customers want to you to move.

Those who go out of business do so usually because they have lost touch with customers. To be successful in marketing, you must absolutely give the market what it requests, not what you think it needs. The market determines what the market wants. The biggest mistake most

33

business owners make is *telling* the market what it wants instead of responding to those wants.

Over the years I have worked and consulted for many companies. I've seen many instances in which an organization performs a market survey and receives feedback.

But then the CEO makes the final decision on what the marketing program (what it looks like, its name, message, etc.) should be! When the sales target is not reached, she wonders why the marketing campaign didn't work. This is because the CEO did not listen to what the market was telling her.

You have no right to determine what the market wants; you just have the obligation to deliver it based on the feedback the market gives you.

Speak with your customers periodically, over the phone or by e-mail, to capture feedback on how they use your product or service, what can be improved to make the experience more pleasurable, and how the company can provide the perceived value it seeks. The best ideas in business always come from customers. You are in business to serve, and the only way to serve effectively is to listen and then deliver.

Most of your competitors have no idea of their customers' opinions and expectations. Why? These companies never take the time to ask! Once you understand what your customers want, you should aim to not only give them what they want but surpass their expectations.

You may have heard the expression, "If you want to double sales, just double the time you spend with customers." Get feedback from them! Why does this work? Spending more time with customers not only provides feedback for product improvement but also allows you to define new product opportunities.

Whenever I speak or give workshops, people tell me what additional support information, resource guides, and other information they'd like. These are products and services I can develop or source for them. Feedback gives me the opportunity to make money because I always get new ideas from customers. If I continue to listen, I become better and do better marketing. Business is a constantly evolving process. It is not static. Your customers evolve, too, and the only way to find out what's going on in their lives is to get feedback and not make assumptions.

If you are not constantly collecting feedback from your customers, you will lose touch with your market, and your product will eventually stop adding value to customers' lives. Your customers will then find someone else who will provide the value they want.

Let's say you sell CDs to students, but you find they're now into MP3s. If you are in constant touch and have constant feedback, you will align your business with changing market needs. Never get complacent; align yourself with the market.

Irrespective of the type or size of a business, feedback can and should always be collected. Get as creative as you want. Set up 1-800 numbers, offer incentives for feedback, or send out questionnaires. The buzzword in marketing today is *immersion studies*. Immerse yourself by spending a day with your customers, and find out how they use your product. Why? When the customers' problems become your problems, you make money.

The only way to find and identify customer problems is through close contact with your clientele. Walk in their shoes. Know how they feel when they do business with you.

Don't guess what customers want. Ask them! Many organizations fear feedback because they think it may be negative. But feedback teaches what should be modified so the business can get on the right track. To get to the right destination, you need the right directions. Feedback allows you to fine-tune your marketing approach.

Feedback is the glue that helps you bond to the market. Feedback is a basic marketing move. Unless you know how the market perceives you, you cannot effectively sell your product or bring value to the marketplace.

Gather feedback by using simple questionnaires. They may or may not be elaborate, depending on the resources of your organization. If you cannot develop a form, simply hand out a business card to each customer with a purchase. The card can read something like: "Thank you for being our customer! Give us feedback, and get 10 percent off your next purchase." Or send an e-mail: "Please take a moment and tell me about your experience doing business with us. Good, bad, or indifferent—we want to know!"

An organization equipped to do so may put a tracking number on a direct mailing. When customers reply by phone, ask for their tracking number and inquire what they found appealing about the mailing. Your customers' replies will tell you how effective your mailing is and how you can make sure people notice it more easily next time.

With today's technology, you can easily implement online surveys. Companies like Surveymonkey and Zoomerang allow you to design a survey that can be e-mailed to customers around the world. For about twenty dollars per month, you can survey as many customers as you like. Reports, which are provided as part of the service, can be used to make independent claims about how you compare to the competition, giving you a competitive edge in a crowded and noisy marketplace.

No matter the size of the company, survey customers by using automated online tools. For just twenty dollars per month, you can find out what they really think!

Black belt marketers survey customers because they know the power of feedback. Feedback makes you and your product more valuable in the eyes of the customer. It makes you a better marketer. To get feedback, of course, you need to know who your customers are, so a database is critical. Move 19 covers the power of databases.

Large corporations often pay thousands of dollars for feedback from customers, and they may stage focus groups or send out survey forms prepared by professional market-research companies. Although the cost of such programs may seem high, it is negligible when you consider

MOVE 6: GET AS MUCH FEEDBACK AS POSSIBLE!

the price of a mistake. Measure twice, and cut once. Get the facts first before making an investment in any formal marketing program, and test your ideas until you have proved that you have a winning concept. Feedback is a directional tool. When you constantly seek feedback and listen to it, failure is unlikely because now you know what to do to be successful. Quality feedback leads to that million-dollar product or service.

Feedback also keeps you honest. It allows you to fine-tune your approach to what works and helps you see where change is needed. It keeps you in touch with your customers and your market. Conduct market surveys regularly, irrespective of your business type. Feedback drives your marketing investment strategy because it tells you what customers value. You can then invest in your marketing with confidence.

All black belt marketers know that "time and distance compound errors." You must get feedback as quickly as possible; this way, you have time to make the corrections necessary without going too far off track. Black belt marketers also believe that "To get to the right destination, you need the right directions." Feedback is basically a series of data points that will lead you to the pot of gold.

Once you get feedback, act on it. I once asked the owner of a carpet cleaning company to name the most important feedback he received from his customers. He said it was hygiene—people get their carpets cleaned because they worry about allergies and bugs. I asked the owner if he used this information in any of his direct mailings and marketing activities. His answer was no. Feedback is like getting gold back into your hands. Take advantage of it!

Amazon.com always sends out a survey after they have shipped their products. They want to know what to do to improve continuously. It's a simple and powerful move that a business of any type and size can use.

Incorporate feedback into the way you market, and you cannot help but become successful. You must have a formal feedback mechanism if you are serious about growing your business.

MOVE

7

Get testimonials

MOVE 7

Get testimonials

Testimonials from satisfied customers are one of the most important assets of any company. Authentic, signed testimonials are more valuable than machinery or buildings. The purpose of marketing is to show value and to help others, and great testimonials are evidence that you did this successfully.

Another way to look at marketing is as a courtroom battle. And in this court, you are trying to defend your product or service. The testimonials function as witnesses, social proof, and evidence that you have delivered your customers' expectations and values. You did not underdeliver or lie. As such, you are innocent!

Words from real-world customers are one of the most powerful marketing weapons you can have. No one can argue with success as long as praise comes from genuine customers. Testimonials make you believable in the world of marketing, and positive feedback is a credit to your organization and you. Be proud of testimonials and share them with as many people as possible. You worked hard for them!

Marketing gurus know the way to handle negative reactions: they show positive outcomes. Use as many testimonials and success stories as possible. You should get a testimonial from each of your clients. Customers always have the final word in any business, and the highest compliment any business can receive is a list of testimonials from satisfied clients.

We already discussed that the major obstacle preventing people from buying is the fear of making a wrong decision. Prospects don't trust that you can give them what they want unless you prove to them that you can. But if they read about someone who has used your product or service and obtained great results, they can decide to buy more confidently.

Testimonials are one of the most underused and overlooked marketing tools available. Any successful business has a list of satisfied clients. But how many companies ask each customer for a testimonial? Testimonials are your pot of gold.

Last night on television I saw a powerful advertisement for a cruise. What made the ad so powerful were the testimonials that appeared throughout. Well-known magazines and newspapers quoted positive experiences. Based on this, I was motivated to at least order some information, because theirs was good social proof.

Some organizations shy away from testimonials because they do not want to seem to boast about what they do. But, as I explained earlier, black belt marketers are aggressive, and they want to protect people. They don't boast; they simply state the facts and are proud to do so.

In the game of marketing, the organization that brings the most value to the market is the one that eventually wins. Testimonials set you apart from any competition. I am more likely to do business with a company that shows me one hundred testimonials than with a company that shows me none. The more testimonials you have, the easier you make it for others to make intelligent purchases.

Now that you're convinced of the power and impact of testimonials, let's talk about what testimonials should say. Testimonials must show the exact result your customers have gained from using your product or service and how it has improved their lives. Testimonials should not just boast how great you are! If I got a testimonial from one of my clients that said, "Ali is a very knowledgeable marketing professional, and we have learned a great deal from him," it would do little because it essentially just brags about me. But what if I asked one of my clients to talk more specifically about how my book affected his or her life? "I used just one of Ali's black belt marketing techniques and increased sales by 60 percent over three months. All with no extra investment! I can't wait to apply some more moves."

This testimonial increases customers' curiosity and makes them want to reap a similar benefit. They see my value for themselves. (By the way, curiosity is a move unto itself: move 42). The most powerful testimonials describe results in highly specific terms. The more specific the description of the outcome, the more valuable the testimonial.

Notice how infomercials use most of the given time for testimonials. They can get customers to reach for the phone mainly through the impact of testimonials.

If you get a good result, then I want the same thing. And you have shown me how I can get it. Having a third-party endorsement gives your organization a lot of credibility, especially if the third party is already well-known, like a famous person or company. Without testimonials, people are asked to buy simply based on faith that they can gain the value they expect.

The more evidence you provide to the judge and jury, the easier it becomes for them to make a decision in your favor. A good testimonial addresses the major objection people have in purchasing from you— lack of trust.

As we discussed, people may not believe you, but they will believe others, especially those whom they know or can relate to. Having other people talk about you is a powerful marketing move. How do you get testimonials? Call your clients, interview them, and ask what they really like about your product or service, then write it up and e-mail the document to them for consent. Tell them you would like to use it as sales literature.

As you can see, you are now quickly gaining some real black belt marketing power.

MOVE
8

Never invest until you test

MOVE 8

Never invest until you test

A powerful move that will grow sales is your ability to make fact-based decisions, which comes through testing and discovering what works. Every great marketer knows the importance of testing. It is one of the foundation pillars of black belt marketing.

Unless you are constantly testing, you have no idea of what is working. You just assume it works. But assumptions in marketing will kill you!

Most businesses assume their prospects can decide for themselves what they should buy. But, remember, people see an average of fifteen thousand to twenty-five thousand advertisements per day. Businesses compete with everyone else for their share of time. Because of the large number of messages—or as most marketing experts call them, "noise"—most people simply ignore all the messages and only focus on those provided through a trusted friend. This is why referrals are the way that most products and services get sold.

Many businesses assume that by running an advertisement, they'll encourage people to buy their product or service, without realizing that consumers, prospects, and potential customers are all looking for education.

GET YOUR BLACK BELT IN MARKETING

Never assume your prospects or customers know anything, and take every opportunity to educate them as to why they should buy from you. But how do you avoid making assumptions about your prospects or your products?

Testing prevents you from making false assumptions. It allows you to find out what works and what doesn't. Unless you test, by default, you are guessing. Testing eliminates the risk of failure through trial and error. It is an experiment, or a safe test.

Black belt marketers find out what works as quickly as possible. Once you find what works, you can start making sound investments in marketing programs that generate revenue for your organization.

Old-School Marketing
Guess
May/May not work

Black Belt Marketing
Test
It works!/It does not work

Only through testing can we determine outcomes with any degree of certainty. And because things change, you need to test all the time. What works well today may not work well tomorrow. The market may have changed, and you need to change with it. A retailer may change a display to attract a higher level of traffic, but is it effective? Testing will show the way.

Whenever I give talks or training programs, I study the response of my audience and can see if they are connected with my content and delivery, usually by looking at the way they are responding to me. After my presentations, I talk to the audience members and listen attentively to what it is they enjoyed most about my presentation. They may like to hear certain words and phrases in a certain way. They may like certain parts of my slides. I make notes at the end, and then I refine my material for the next presentation. This way, I am continuously testing and getting better. Testing my audience gives me new ideas for reports, products, or books. Because I have tested, I know what they want! Here's a secret that will help you in marketing:

48

MOVE 8: NEVER INVEST UNTIL YOU TEST

ABT = ALWAYS BE TESTING!

Here's a marketing riddle:

"How do you cut your advertising budget in half?"
"Get twice the response from the same ad."

But how can you double the response from the same ad? Through testing, of course. If you are running an advertisement, make minor changes to see how the response changes. You will immediately see the power of testing. Here are some of the things that you may want to test:

- The headline
- The body copy
- The day of the week the ad runs
- The use of graphics and pictures
- The opening sentence
- The position of the ad on the page
- The call to action

You will never appreciate the power of testing unless you try it for yourself. If the same advertisement generates more revenue at no extra cost, you have maximized your spending on advertising.

Black belt marketers live and die by the word *leverage*. Leverage is defined as the ability to do a lot with a little. Each of your marketing activities should focus on generating the maximum revenue possible with minimal effort. Testing is a very powerful tool for you to gain leverage.

Testing is your passport to millions. Once you find what works, you have struck gold. Then you can duplicate it and scale it into a money-making machine. This is how McDonald's, Howard Johnson hotels, and other famous franchises have made billions of dollars. A franchise is no more than a system that produces reproducible results. A franchise is a tested and validated concept.

GET YOUR BLACK BELT IN MARKETING

Everything in marketing can be tested. Here are some examples:

- The headline to an e-mail
- The way you greet a customer
- The way you make a sales presentation
- The response from a mailing
- Where the ads appear in a journal

What gets a great response? What works? What doesn't? Starting today, test every marketing activity that you do, make changes, and test again. You will soon realize just how ineffective some of your marketing has been. There is always room for improvement.

You may have heard of people who ran tiny classified ads, found them to work, and then ran them across America and became millionaires! Because they understood the power of testing, they tested a small advertisement. Once they found that it brought in sales, they are able to adjust their model to a larger-scaled operation.

In marketing you have no right to decide what the market wants, just the obligation to deliver it. How do you find out what the market wants? You need to test.

Management consulting has a concept called BDP: best demonstrated practice. These strategies have been tested and are proven recipes for success. They simply find out what the best way to solve a particular business problem is, then they apply this to another business situation.

The best way to learn anything new is to imitate the best. If you want to learn real estate, study how Donald Trump does deals. Some call this modeling or mirroring time-tested and proven strategies. Success leaves clues. If you do something that has worked for someone else, it means that it has been tested and will work for you when you do exactly the same steps. It is a recipe for success. The next time you see an advertisement that appeals to you, consider adapting it to your particular product or service. Put it to the test!

MOVE 8: NEVER INVEST UNTIL YOU TEST

The most revolutionary marketing ideas come from taking well-proven and tested existing concepts and applying these to new areas. The ball point pen came from the roll-on deodorant.

Top companies hire experienced executives. Who are these people? They are folks who have already been successful at launching products, implementing new accounting systems, or making major accomplishments in an organization. They know with a high degree of predictability what to do and what works. How did they gain this experience? Though trial and error, by figuring out what works and what doesn't. Corporations pay these people top dollar because they can save a lot of time and money. They use something called OPE (other people's experience), which is nothing more than testing. The people that they hire have already handled situations that they are likely to encounter, have tested and tried different approaches, and know what works and what doesn't. As they say, experience is what you get when you don't get the result you expect!

The shortcut to testing is to find out what someone else is doing in another area of business and then adapting and adopting the same practice. Some of the world's smartest marketers borrow proven concepts from other businesses and apply them to their own. For example, Federal Express' hub-and-spoke business model was born out of the banks' clearinghouse system.

The world's greatest copywriters borrow, adapt, and adopt headlines proven to work from other advertisements in the past. This is perfectly fine, because headlines are not copyrighted material. If you want to know how to write great headlines, just stop at a newsstand and look at all the magazines. Notice how they get your attention in a matter of seconds. The best are *Business Week, Time, Newsweek*, and the *National Enquirer*. The people who write these headlines are some of the world's best marketers. These headlines have been tested and proven to get your attention. You can borrow, adapt, and adopt these headlines to your business. Visit Amazon.com and look at the titles of the best sellers. They tell you what appeals to the market today.

GET YOUR BLACK BELT IN MARKETING

This may surprise you, but marketing folks don't necessarily have all the answers. We can't see the future and don't know what will work. But through testing, we can quickly find out. Testing gives insight. And once you know what works, all you need to do is scale.

A simple change in the headline of an advertisement can increase the response rate by twenty-one times. That is 2,100 percent! It's a proven marketing fact. But what word changes need to be made? Test it. The headline is actually the advertisement of the advertisement.

Testing can usually give you a clear advantage in the marketplace over your competition.

Hardly any advertising agencies today work strictly on commission. That's because they don't know whether the promotions they develop will be successful. If they truly knew what worked, they would be stupid not to work commission rather than a flat fee. Herein lies one of the biggest secrets to marketing: Marketing professionals do not know if what you propose will work (although many claim they do). If we did, we would be the richest people on the planet. At the end of the day, it is the market that will make a final decision; it is the judge and jury. Find out what the market values by testing it. Once you do, you are on your way to success!

Nearly all marketing professionals have some marketing skill, such as doing market research, writing creative copy, designing, and so forth. But none of them knows any better than you do what is going to work. You must learn to trust yourself! Before investing in, duplicating, or scaling any idea, validate it. Validation comes through testing.

How many times have you said, "That will never work"? Remember, it is not for you to say, it is for the market to decide.

The quickest way to find out what your market thinks is to test. And the quicker you can test, the better your chances of success. Those in the pharmaceutical industry often say, "Fail early, fail often—Just find out what works as quickly as possible!" It takes about ten years and several

52

million dollars to develop drugs seen on the pharmacy shelves. Major pharmaceutical companies test quickly to determine whether a certain compound will work. If not, they try another one.

A dentist friend of mine used to run quarter page ads, which got two new customers to call every day. Then she cut the ad size in half and still got two people a day to call. She saved a lot of money by testing.

Fortunately for you, it is highly unlikely that your competition is doing any testing. By testing new ideas and finding out what works, you will be light-years ahead of them. Find what currently brings in the revenue for you, make small changes to the process, and see what happens. The person who makes the most money in business is the one who finds a marketing program that works and then expands it.

Always remember, you have no right to assume what the market wants, just the obligation to deliver what it values. As a trained black belt marketer, *assume nothing and always test before you invest. You test very quickly, using a small amount of money and time, and once you find out what works, you invest your time and money with confidence in what you know works.*

Next time you take a flight, notice how when the plane lands you feel a quick application of the braking methods. Why does this happen so quickly when they have such a long runway? Because they don't assume the brakes are going to work; they test first. If the brakes don't work, they immediately take off again. A false assumption could be fatal. The same applies in the world of marketing.

The other day, my wife showed me some expired pizza coupons that my children had won through a reading program at the local library over the summer. She was about to throw them away. She assumed they were expired, and so they had no value. I told her to test, not guess. I went down to the pizza store, and they took the expired coupons. We got a free pizza!

GET YOUR BLACK BELT IN MARKETING

Not testing is a suicide marketing strategy. It is no different from gambling, and the odds are not in your favor. Failing to test is a trap that many companies without good marketing counsel fall into. Only when you find out what works can you make secure investments.

Most companies are not really playing the game of marketing; they are only practicing. You can only play if you keep score (i.e., get feedback of what is working or not working). Only when you keep score and get feedback, can you improve your game. And this comes through testing.

Master this move alone, and you are well on your way to taking out your competition and earning your black belt in marketing with high honors.

MOVE

9

Always differentiate

MOVE 9

Always differentiate

This move returns us to the fundamentals of marketing. Whatever it takes, be different. Theodore Levitt, a Harvard Business School marketing professor, was one of the first marketing people to point out the importance of being different. This later resulted in other marketers coining the term USP, or unique selling proposition. Being different is a move used by all world-class marketing professionals. Let's look at an example of a USP, and the power it can have. FedEx rose to great heights with this tag line: "When it absolutely, positively has to be there overnight, choose FedEx."

A few words can change the destiny of a business.

A USP sets you apart from the clutter and noise. People have so many choices these days, and it is difficult to differentiate between the alternatives. A unique selling proposition sets you apart from the crowd, and lets people know why you are different. Leading businesses are not necessarily better; they simply are seen or perceived by the market to be better. They are clearly differentiated, usually with a clear USP. In fact, it is more important to be different than to be better.

GET YOUR BLACK BELT IN MARKETING

The term *USP* is well understood in the world of marketing. But as a black belt marketer, you will modify the USP into a UVP (unique value proposition) because you know what people buy at the end of the day is the value they can gain from your product or service. To understand the UVP a bit better, let's study a few real-world examples of businesses that add value by being clearly differentiated.

Business type	Unique value proposition (UVP)
Cell phone companies	Extra minutes, additional phones, fewer dropped calls
Smog testing station	Free tank of gas with a smog test
Cereals	Free gifts inside the cereal box
Hotels	Free Internet, manager's reception, complimentary breakfast
Car rentals	Pick clients up at home
Dry cleaning	Use of special solvents
Airport parking	Free car wash
Mortgage broker	BMW with a mortgage
Furniture stores	No payment for two years
Oil change	Includes a car wash. Done in thirty minutes or your money back!
Magazines	Free CD (Recorded interviews)
Clothing store	Broad range of products/brands

Restaurant	Best service, offer cookbooks
Mail order company	Free delivery to loyal customers advanced customer service
Chocolates	Different packaging
Electrician	Membership in Better Business Bureau and other associations

Black belt marketing is about being seen as different. If your product or service is not seen as different in the market, people will revert to buying on price because your product or service will be viewed as a commodity. A commodity, by definition, means that there is no differentiation.

Notice in the above examples how the differentiation may not be huge. In fact, the factor that makes your product or service different may be simple and subtle. But it should be enough to give the business a winning edge. Always think how your product or service is better and how you can add more value to your customers than anyone else. My UVP is "I am marketing for everybody, including you!"

Most marketing gurus focus on marketing for sales or business growth. I believe marketing is too powerful to be contained in the business world. I believe in the universality of marketing. I see the marketing world in color, whereas others see it in black and white. I would like to see as many people as possible benefit from the power that marketing offers.

I have a goal to write one new marketing book per year. Ten years from now, by default, I will become one of the world's experts in marketing. Not because I am any smarter or better than anyone else, but because I will have clearly differentiated myself from other marketing people. I have already achieved 20 percent of my goal.

If you want to understand differentiation better, just look at your cereal box in the morning. Notice how the cereals for kids have games on the back or have toys in them. Kids ask their parents to buy cereal for the value added games and toys. These items help to differentiate these cereals from all the other cereal boxes out there.

Anything and everything should and can be differentiated. Differentiation gives you the winning edge. It is the one step further that allows you to win the game. People always buy based on the value they perceive to be getting. The differentiation doesn't even have to be related to the product or service. It can be completely unrelated, such as offering a free movie ticket to people who buy a certain amount.

Marketing is not an event. It is a process. You must continually look for ways to add value to your product or service. Make your offer more attractive and appealing, and keep doing this.

Domino's Pizza clearly stood above the crowd by saying they offered hot and tasty pizza in thirty minutes or your money back.

This is why education is one of the most powerful forms of marketing. By educating your market, you continually tell them how you are different from the crowd. Once they see this, they will trust you more than anyone else.

To see the power that differentiation has in marketing, just look around you.

We all do not wear the same clothes, so why should our products be the same? Whatever it takes, be different, be better, be unique. When you are different, you will get noticed.

The most successful products are the most differentiated ones, according to Jack Trout, the marketer who wrote an excellent book called *Differentiate or Die.*

The act of being able to differentiate yourself quickly is an act of adding value. The more differentiation, the more superior you will be in the marketplace. I have written two books on marketing. Any marketing professional could write a book on marketing. The only difference is that I did.

An electrician may hold professional membership in an association. It shows the customers he takes the work seriously and is looking for ways to enhance competency. The market will now view him at a higher level than someone not in an association.

A dentist I know runs ads in the yellow pages, and it keeps her phone ringing. Why? She uses "emergency dental care" as a headline. If you open the yellow pages because you are in pain, it is an emergency. Not one of the other dental ads in those yellow pages uses the word emergency.

People miss the obvious. Open the yellow pages, look at the ads in your category, then create a headline that differentiates your business. Make it large and bold, and listen to your phone ring. Creative headlines are a move unto themselves, which we will be discussing shortly.

Once you have a UVP (unique value proposition), incorporate it into your marketing messaging. Let everyone know why they should choose your product or service over someone else's. How is your product different? The UVP is a small thing that makes the world of difference in marketing.

MOVE

10

Use referrals

MOVE 10

Use referrals

Word of mouth or referrals is the oldest form of marketing in the world. In the Garden of Eden, Eve got Adam to eat the apple based on her recommendation. If you combined all other major marketing vehicles—formal advertising, public relations, press releases, and so on—they would not have the impact that word of mouth has. If you want to generate sales revenue quickly, this move is for you. Study it carefully.

One of the greatest marketing expenses of any business is the cost of acquiring new customers. This can be reduced, and many times eliminated, by using referrals. Referral-based selling is much more effective than conventional selling. It is more effective because most people do not trust salespeople but do trust someone they know, usually a colleague or friend.

Word of mouth is about leveraging one of your most important assets: existing customers. It turns your customers into a twenty-four-hour, seven-day, fifty-two-week no-cost sales force. As a black belt marketer, you know every marketing activity must have an impact. People may glance at a handful of ads, but they will seriously review a word-of-mouth recommendation.

GET YOUR BLACK BELT IN MARKETING

Word of mouth is the silent killer of the competition. If people talk about your product or service in a positive way, they are silently killing the competition. Word of mouth is an invisible force that will eventually take out your competition.

Black belt marketers work on facts, not fiction. They know that about 68 percent of all business is done on a recommendation from someone. So this is where black belt marketers focus 68 percent of the marketing effort.

Most of your competitors claim they get referrals. In a small business, up to 90 percent of all business comes through referrals. But how many people get referrals through a formal and systematic program that proactively gets referrals, instead of just taking what comes in? Do you ask each of your customers for referrals? Or do you just hope they will tell others about your product?

With the right referral system, word about your business will spread like wildfire. If five leading experts in your field recommend your service or product to their database, you will immediately climb to number one in your field.

Referrals level the field. Referrals allow smaller businesses to take on large corporate organizations with huge advertising budgets. It is not the Internet that levels the field in marketing. It is word of mouth. Study some of the most successful companies in the world, and you will find word-of-mouth marketing is a key part of their success. Referrals get people talking and create a buzz.

Gmail never advertised. Their marketing was done by word of mouth, with a link to pass on invitations to friends. Apple did not formally advertise for several years because its word-of-mouth marketing worked so well. People loved the product and wanted to share their experiences with others.

Statistics from the American Marketing Association show it is five times more difficult to get new customers than to get business from existing customers. This clearly shows where black belt marketers should focus their efforts. Let your competitors go out and chase new customers, while you bring them in with a formal referral system that converts word of mouth into sales.

All business owners claim they have a referral system, but if you ask, is it any of the following?

- Disciplined
- Systematic
- Measured
- Monitored
- Tracked
- Consistent

The answer is frequently no. Many business owners assume referrals will turn up, instead of having a system to get them. Referrals are the primary source of customers for most businesses. Referral based customers;

- Are already well-qualified prospects
- Buy fast because they already trust you
- Don't haggle on price
- Refer you more
- Buy the most

Books have been written about how to use referrals to generate sales. Implemented correctly, systematic, formal referral systems can easily be used to double sales. Acquiring referrals is a never-ending process because as long as clients keep referring, your business will keep growing! It simply compounds.

Referrals allowed me to double the sales of two start-up companies for which I worked. If you do a good job, people are more than willing to help you. Just ask with confidence because you gave them the perceived value they expect.

GET YOUR BLACK BELT IN MARKETING

Look at the math: Referral is the compound interest of marketing. If one customer refers two new customers, and this continues, how many customers would you have in just twenty days? One million!

1
2
4
8
16
32
64
128
256
512
1,024
2,048
4,096
8,192
16,384
32,768
65,536
131,072
262,144
524,288
1,048,576

Another way to recognize the power of referrals is to ask yourself how quickly you could let everyone in America know about your product or service. If one person tells twenty-five people, and then each of those people tell twenty-five more, six times over, then all of America will have heard about your product or service.

Events	People
1	25
2	625
3	15,625

4	390,625
5	9.765.625
6	244,140,625

When people tell me they want a 10 to 12 percent increase in sales, I tell them it's easy. Get each of your current customers to refer two people to you over one year. If only half of the people they refer become customers, you still double your sales!

Of course you've heard the old adage, "Birds of a feather flock together." Each of your customers knows people similar to them. Give them permission to spread the word! Ask each of your existing customers for referrals. If you do not, you limit the sales revenue you deserve. Some of my clients ask me what to do if people do not give referrals. I teach them to use move 6—get feedback. Now these clients have feedback to make corrections. Referrals are a great mechanism to capture feedback.

Marketing experts agree that word-of-mouth or referral-based marketing is about a thousand times more effective than conventional advertising.

On average, the American public is exposed to fifteen thousand ads per day. How many products do you buy as a result? Yet if someone calls and recommends a product or service, you will be much more likely to buy.

People usually buy based on recommendations, because they trust that the information from a friend or relative is accurate. Referrals allow you to hit home runs easily. All you need are key influencers to promote your product or service to other people. Key influencers are people that are known and respected in your particular business. They are people that have a large following, or network.

Another way to look at referrals is with the sphere of influence. It is estimated that most people know at least ten people. Let us consider that one person is extremely satisfied with your product and tells ten people about it. If these ten people continue to tell another ten people about you every week, here is what happens:

$$10 \times 10 = 100$$
$$100 \times 10 = 1,000$$
$$1,000 \times 10 = 10,000$$
$$10,000 \times 10 = 100,000$$
$$100,000 \times 10 = 1,000,000$$
$$1,000000 \times 10 = 10,000,000$$

In six weeks you will have ten million new prospects that have the potential to be converted into paying customers!

All these examples show why referrals are a proven black belt strategy. The exponential growth that referrals provide can weaken your competition. Word of mouth rapidly decreases the marketing cost and increases the effectiveness of marketing. Getting customers to sell for you is the most powerful and under-utilized marketing technique known.

The hardest part of marketing today is to get people's attention.

- E-mails have spam filters
- TiVo allows us to cut out ads
- Caller ID and voicemail cut out telemarketers
- CDs or MP3s are listened to in the car instead of radio ads
- Junk mail is thrown out without ever being opened
- Pop-up blockers prevent unsolicited ads

But people will always listen to the recommendations of a friend or trusted advisor. Word of mouth is the only guaranteed way to cut through the marketing clutter.

Did you know that Post-it failed during the product launch but succeeded through word of mouth? The marketing began when 3M gave them out to secretaries and administrators. Soon everyone was talking about them, and the rest is history.

Word of mouth works so well because people are busy. If someone tells you what works, you don't have to wade through all the products or services that don't work.

We don't live in the information age. We live in the age of information overload. We have to take a lot of information and make it relevant and useful to us. This is why brokers are well paid. They have already done the legwork.

Many marketing professionals will ask for referrals only once. But the black belt marketers ask for referrals every three months. If your product or service is a good value, feel confident in continually asking your customers for more referrals. Never stop asking for referrals.

Give your clients the tools they need to spread the good word. Most organizations do not have formal referral systems, and few actually give their customers information about their companies. Give each client a starter kit to help new prospects understand what you do and the value you can add. This includes samples, presentations, literature, or other information new prospects would like to know. Give your loyal customers or clients the same information you would give to your sales force. After all, your clients are now your extended sales force. Your clients want to look good in front of their friends. It is your duty to give them the tools. By doing so, the word will soon start to spread about your product or service, and this is what black belt marketing is all about.

MOVE
11

It's all about you, you, you

MOVE 11

It's all about you, you, you

You now know that marketing is about others, but how do we let other people know that we are concerned about their well-being? Use the most powerful word in the marketing dictionary: you.

Study the text below. It's a real example from an advertisement run by the Learning Annex in April 2007

> Have **you** seen the hot new movie *The Secret*? This sensational film is currently exploding around the world. It's the most powerful lesson in personal growth I've ever learned. If you've seen it, **you** know how amazing it is. And if **you** haven't seen it yet, nothing should stop **you** from checking it out.
>
> Would **you** like to learn The Secret Laws of Attraction from the stars of the movie? The Learning Annex Real Estate & Wealth Expo has just added Secret teachers from the movie to train **you** to attract anything using the laws of automatic prosperity. What would your life be like if **you** could accomplish anything—*and everything*—**you** want? Would **you** buy a bigger house? Would **you** start your own business? Would

you take a year off and travel the world? Once **you** learn The Secret Laws of Attraction, **you** will change your life forever!

Now, let me ask you a question. Did you find this text compelling? Did it excite you? How would you rate it out of ten? Notice the word you was used no less than fifteen times in this copy. The word you makes the copy personal and customized. Although it went out to several million people, it talked to each of them on a personal or one-to-one basis.

The three-letter word *you* makes the reader feel important. It makes them connect with the author and makes the message both personal and relevant. So the next move to master as you advance to your black belt in marketing is to use the word you as frequently as possible in any form of marketing communication or presentation. Remember in marketing it's all about others, and you is the word used to connect with others.

You is the most powerful word in the marketing dictionary. It is subliminal, so people will not even notice how many times you use it, but it is persuasive. It shows people you want to add value for them and gets them connected to you. This secret has been guarded by marketing professionals for centuries, and it's made millions for those who understand it. Let's look at another example of how using the word you turns the tables.

> *"Our company offers software for home-based financial analysis. It's good for a small family that's never done a budget. It is easy to use and perfect for people who have never used software."*

Versus

> *"If you are looking for a solution for your home-based financial budgeting needs, you need to look no further. You can try XYZ software free for thirty days in your home. See for yourself the change it makes, and then you decide. Call us at ..."*

MOVE 11: IT'S ALL ABOUT YOU, YOU, YOU

Notice how the meaning changes and becomes much more powerful, simply by planting the word you several times in the text.

Let's try it one more time, so you can really master this move.

> *"I can show you how you can double your income. Give me just twenty minutes of your time a month. Would you like to learn more?"*

Is this powerful? Why? Do you think that you would want to learn more? Of course, because I used the word you no less than five times.

Maybe you had an English teacher who taught you not to use the same word twice in a sentence. This is the opposite of what I teach! I never did well in English at school, but I have done exceptionally well in marketing. Quality marketers break grammar rules!

The ability to write good marketing copy is a skill of top marketers, and they can charge up to $25,000 just for one sales letter because they know how to get people engaged by using the word you!

Just hope your competitors had a great English teacher. Most people write grammatically correct marketing copy, using the English they were taught in school. It may earn them an A but may not help sell anything. Because they are more concerned about the grammar than the readers' response, the copy may come across as boring and may not connect with people.

Try this concept and you will be amazed at the response you get from customers. Even "thank you," has the word you in it! Also notice how this book's title emphasizes getting your black belt. I worded it this way to impart a sense of ownership. I wrote it for you.

In fact, the next time you read a sales proposition that appeals to you, take a highlighter and highlight how many times the word you or your is used. You will gain insight into how this magical three-letter word has made marketing professionals millions.

Black belt marketers know that the more relevant the message is to you, the more impact it will have.

The best marketing copy or communication has the word you all over it. Make it a part of your habitual vocabulary, and both prospects and customers will be attracted to you!

MOVE
12

Hook up with good transmitters

MOVE 12

Hook up with good transmitters

Most business owners feel they need to go it alone when it comes to building a customer base. But acquiring initial customers is the hardest challenge for any business.

The quickest, most effective, and most powerful way to acquire customers is to partner with someone who already has the people you need to reach. Different terms can be used to describe this relationship: Some call it a partnership, others call it an affiliate relationship, and yet others a joint venture. But the method is basically networking, which is powerful. Hook up with people who can transmit your message quickly to your desired audience.

It costs money to get customers; they certainly do not turn up free. Find someone already talking to the people you need to reach, and offer them a strong incentive to give you access to their customers or database. By doing so, you can build a customer base quickly. You may even offer 100 percent of the profits from the first sale, because, once you get a customer, they may continue to buy. You can then make all the money on the back-end (the residual or ongoing profit over the years).

Here are important things to remember when networking:

1. Find people respected and known to the people you want to reach.

2. Make them an offer they cannot refuse.

3. Provide all the information they need.

4. Ensure the accounting is done correctly.

For example, if I want to sell one of my sales audio programs, I would identify some top sales trainers that I respect by doing a search on the Internet. I would tell them that I would be happy to give them 50 percent of the profit made on any sale of my CD at their events. I would ensure that my product is delivered and available at their events. We would ensure that we both understood the monthly statements.

This type of arrangement is certainly not easy, and it takes time. People need to trust that you have something of value for their customers. They have spent a lot of time building relationships with this customer base and need to feel you are a value-add. But you're a black belt marketer, a master at showing people value. And one such deal can take your sales through the roof! As you become well-known, people will soon approach you! It works both ways!

It's immensely powerful to have well-known and respected companies promoting for you. Initially, you may have doubts, but, when you consider the cost to acquire new customers, it is a no-brainer. You can get to a lot more customers by leveraging someone else's relationship instead of going it alone. Even the Lone Ranger did not go alone!

13

Know the ultimate marketing success formula: M = M×M×M

MOVE 13

Know the ultimate marketing success formula: M = M×M×M

E arly on we laid the foundation of marketing. I trained you how to focus on the perceived value others want. In this move, we are going to learn the ultimate marketing success formula that only a black belt marketer would know.

To ensure your marketing is effective, all you need to do is to get the right message to the right market, using the right medium. This is done using the Marketing Triad. or M x M x M

Message	=	Value Proposition
Messenger	=	Vehicle
Market	=	The person that can most benefit from the message

MESSAGE
The message is your unique value proposition, (Move #9). It is the reason why someone would gain immense benefit and value from what you are offering. As you now know, marketing is all about value that others can gain from your offering. It shows them the pay–off, or per-

ceived value to them. As a Black belt marketer, you know how to make powerful value propositions. You do this by using the "Godfather marketing strategy"—making people offers that they cannot refuse.

For instance, if you are trying to become a best-selling author, you would offer your book for twenty dollars, but people get one thousand dollars worth of free bonuses if they buy your book. As long as this message is delivered to the right person, there is no reason why they would not take you up on your offer

MESSENGER

The messenger is the vehicle that you choose to deliver your message. When traditional marketers think of marketing, they usually think of the messenger, or vehicle. Television, radio, print, the Internet, billboards— are all examples of messengers. The messenger simply takes your message and puts it in the hands of the people most likely to benefit from it.

MARKET

The market is a person or a group of people that would be most likely to benefit from your message. Black belt marketing uses a process called "market segmentation" to focus in on the market. Market segmentation is a very powerful tool that allows marketers to home in on hot prospects, or people most likely to gain value by receiving the message.

A good way to look at market segmentation is like ZIP codes. If I wanted to get a letter delivered to your house, and you told me that your ZIP was 94521, I would arrive in Concord, California, but if you said it was 94521-56432, I would be able to deliver it to your exact house!

As you can see, the ultimate marketing success formula is no more than basic common sense. If you get your message to someone that can gain value from it by using the right messenger, then there is no reason why they would not take you up on it. As I said in the introduction, I am going to teach you the power of logic and simplicity.

MOVE 13: KNOW THE ULTIMATE MARKETING SUCCESS FORMULA: M = M×M×M

The message is the value proposition. Tell people clearly how you can add value to their lives. Solve their problems and improve their lives. The messenger is the vehicle you choose to deliver your message.

The market is the group of people that can benefit the most from the message. If you have the right message targeted to the right market and delivered with the right messenger, you are a winner!

Here are some examples of messengers that people often use:
- Internet
- Radio
- Television
- Newspapers
- Telephone
- Direct Mailings

These are simply the vehicles.

This equation $M = M \times M \times M$ is very well understood by successful marketing professionals, but you may see it in different ways:

Marketing = Message x Messenger x Market

Cannon Ball × Cannon
Message × Movement
Value × Volume
Impact × Quantity
Message × Medium
Offer × List
Valuable × Visible
Sales Tools × Sales People
Exposure × Exposure time

All the above combinations assume that both the message and messenger are focused on the right market. They all break down into the following components:

GET YOUR BLACK BELT IN MARKETING

1. A sound message or value proposition—the reason someone would be interested in listening to you—Message

2. This message must be delivered using the right delivery vehicle—Messenger

3. The message must be targeted and delivered to the people that are going to gain the most from the message—Market

True marketing is a mix of message and medium and market

The message in marketing is the UVP—unique value proposition (move 9). Without a sound, tested, robust value proposition, you cannot be effective. Have you heard the saying, "Don't kill the messenger"? You wouldn't want to kill the messenger if he had something of value to say. If the messenger does not bring a message of value, then the marketing is ineffective. When there is no value in the message, it ends up in the trash can, no matter who the messenger may be.

Many of the great names in marketing were initially copywriters. These include David Ogilvy, Claude Hopkins, and Jay Conrad Levinson. They are professional wordsmiths who know how to write world-class copy. Many of them worked for advertising agencies.

Although most people associate marketing with the medium (television, radio, print), it's the message that makes the difference in marketing. Black belt marketers know how to write quality copy. As marketers, we do not control the medium or messengers, but we do control the message—the quality and content.

The way to write quality copy is to capture feedback from customers: what they like and what appeals to them. Listen to what your customers say. They will do your writing for you.

This ultimate marketing formula is universal. If you are looking for a job, all you need to do is get your value proposition to the decision maker using a network contact. If you get your value proposition, or the reason that someone should hire you, to the person that can most benefit from it and do this using a network contact, your success is almost guaranteed.

MOVE 13: KNOW THE ULTIMATE MARKETING SUCCESS FORMULA: M = M×M×M

I show you in my book *Marketing is King!* how my students have gotten job interviews in less than thirty minutes using this exact formula. You can also see their testimonials on my Web site, as proof that it works.

In the case of job hunting,

"Value Proposition" (VP)	=	Message
"Decision Maker" (DM)	=	Market
"Network Contact" (NC)	=	Messenger

So the formula is universal!

Ensure you have the correct balance of quality message combined with the right medium to get your message to the intended audience in large quantities. Like anything in life, marketing is about balance. For an effective marketing campaign, you need:

1. A great message

2. A great messenger

3. Both used in the right proportions and delivered to the right audience.

You can choose from literally thousands of messengers. Hundreds of thousands of magazines, television, radio stations, and billboards exist in the United States alone. Which should you choose to get to the right audience? What should your message be? I don't know. Test what works for your product or service (move 8). When you figure it out, you are on your way to making a serious amount of money!

MOVE

14

Use powerful headlines

MOVE 14

Use powerful headlines

Why is it called headline news? Because headlines get your attention. The mere fact that you are reading this book shows the power a headline can have. The headline I chose shows prospective readers that I mean business. Readers do not see a marketing book with theoretical and academic information, instead, they see one that cuts through all the hype and gets to the point.

Get Your *Black Belt in Marketing*
81 Power Moves to outperform, outmaneuver, and
outsmart the competition!

The headline advertises the advertisement.

The headline is the first thing you read, and it makes you want to learn more. Any businessperson serious about buying a marketing book wants immediate results and probably doesn't have much time for theory and academic views of marketing. Perhaps they have cash flow problems or creditors calling, and the only way to fight their way out is though black belt marketing. An aggressive title gets attention and stands out from the crowd. That's what black belt marketers do—they perform at a totally different level.

GET YOUR BLACK BELT IN MARKETING

The way to become good at writing headlines is simple. Write down headlines that appeal to you, whether in newspapers, in the mail, on television, or on radio. Keep these headlines in a notebook. Within weeks, you will have a list of some of the finest headlines ever written. You can then change, adapt, or adopt these headlines to your business, product, or service. Headlines cannot be copyrighted, and you will be using them in a different context.

Knowing how to write powerful headlines is a skill every black belt marketer must acquire. Even your e-mail subject line is a headline, and 99 percent of people open e-mails based on the headline.

Remember, marketing is about communicating value, and a headline is the summary of it.

MOVE
15

Set up an e-newsletter

15

Set up an e-newsletter

A s part of your black belt training, revisit the fundamentals. This simple act will keep your marketing effective and your efforts productive. Let's review two marketing fundamentals:

1. WHY DO PEOPLE BUY PRODUCTS AND SERVICES?

People buy products and services to improve the quality of life. When they see what you offer has the capability to do this, they buy. When they believe your offering is the best choice over all the alternatives, they buy. Once your prospects feel understood, you will get the sale. Your product or service should provide hope and a sense of optimism that it will enhance life! Your solution should provide both economic and emotional value.

2. HOW SHOULD YOU SELL?

Now that we know how people buy, we come to the obvious question: How should you sell?

GET YOUR BLACK BELT IN MARKETING

The black belt marketer sells not by selling but by helping people buy. She helps others make informed and intelligent decisions. Black belt marketers are educators.

Notice how black belt marketers do the opposite of what other marketers do. Instead of selling, they simply help people buy the product or service they believe will give their customers an edge in life. In reality, we can never sell anything to anyone; we can only help them buy. The same concept, incidentally, applies to management: we cannot manage anyone; we can only give direction and leadership.

So why did I detail why people buy and how to sell? Because this fundamental marketing knowledge helps us to create constant and consistent messaging with your market, which builds trust. The best vehicle to accomplish this is through an e-newsletter. Some marketing experts use the term value item. An e-newsletter is an example of a value item, something that brings value to others.

When sales are down, examine your marketing. When was the last time you were in contact with your market? People buy from you because they trust you offer the best solution. So the number one way to develop trust is through consistent communication. Remembering the adage, "Out of sight, out of mind" will help you realize why newsletters work so well. Newsletters help you build a brand.

Marketing is simply a battle for the mind. For example, branding is a powerful tool; customers choose a brand because it implies a sense of security and protection and a promise to deliver. A brand is simply a promise.

Black belt marketers know they cannot control the timing, but they can control the value. When people can see the value your product or service can bring through the communication you provide, then, when the time comes to buy, you will be the first person they call. Here's an example: A carpet cleaning service sends a monthly e-newsletter to customers that points out the importance of hygiene and stresses how pollens and dust in carpets are a major source for allergies. When the time comes for the prospect to clean his carpet, that marketer will get the sale. The carpet cleaner is clearly differentiated in the minds of the buyer. The carpet cleaning service has built trust through the process of continual education.

Many services can set up automated e-mail mailings for newsletters. They provide the template; you provide the content and timing. One of them, GOT Corporation, is used by some of America's major corporations, including Yahoo and Salesforce.com. For about $25 per month, you can set up an automated e-newsletter mailing to 2,500 people.

So how should a newsletter be set up?

1. The content must be informational and educational, not a promotional piece. Your goal is to establish yourself as the expert, the trusted person to go to when a customer or prospect has a problem your product or service can potentially solve. Include as many tips, tricks, and how-tos as possible. You want a prospect to say, "If I can learn so much from a newsletter, what if I actually bought the product or service?"

2. Ensure your Web address and contact details appear many times in the newsletter.

3. Offer incentives, coupons, and other promotional offers.

4. Provide a "refer to a friend" link, and add an opt-out. GOT Corporation and others can help you do this.

5. Follow spam-mailing guidelines. Only mail to an opt-in list (those who have agreed to permission-based marketing).

The primary goal for an e-newsletter is to build a brand for your product or service, so your product's name comes to mind when a customer needs what you offer. You have spent time educating them and showing your expertise. You are now no longer a product or service, you are a brand. And the receivers of your newsletter are no longer prospects or customers; they are clients. Build a relationship through constant communication, and your prospects will trust you can solve their problems.

GET YOUR BLACK BELT IN MARKETING

Product	RELATIONSHIP ⟶	Brand
Prospect / Customer	RELATIONSHIP ⟶	Client

Black belt marketers sell brands to clients. Conventional marketers sell products to customers. What's the difference? Black belt marketers have established relationships for what they have to offer and to whom they offer it.

The concept of an e-newsletter is the basis of black belt marketing: education- based selling. Why are e-newsletters guaranteed to be successful?

1. You can monitor results of e-newsletters to get the statistics on your campaign, using the GOT software. See what works, and change the approach as necessary. A system to reach up to 2,500 people for about $25 is quite cost-effective!

2. The best businesses have the deepest level of relationship (a following) with clients. They keep clients informed and educated. In return, these clients are loyal and willing to refer to others.

3. People always read information of value to them.

4. The best marketers in the world do not do much formal or traditional marketing, such as advertising. However, they are continually in touch with their database, building long-term and lasting relationships.

Black belt marketers know relationship is everything. The black belt moves in the book funnel down to building relationships and improving the lives of others. This is what a black belt marketer does.

MOVE
16

Commit to a marketing function

16

Commit to a marketing function

How do you increase the sales of a company? Become a black belt marketer. Marketing is about bringing value to the marketplace. Quality marketing makes selling easy and, ideally, unnecessary.

Marketing is the only function in a business that can increase sales. Every other function in a company is a cost center.

Marketing = Money

Without a sale, no revenue comes into a company, and without a sale, no one has anything to do in a company because no products or services need to be delivered. Sales are the heart of any company. It is what keeps it alive. The ability to generate sales is a significant factor in the valuation of a company. In most cases, a company's values are based on discounted cash flow. Once investors see a company has the ability to be a generate cash, they see the opportunity to make money. Marketing generates these sales, which in turn generates cash. Drive sales by showing others the value they gain by doing business with you.

Marketing = Perceived Value

GET YOUR BLACK BELT IN MARKETING

The only way to grow a business is to bring value to the marketplace. Either learn marketing as a sole proprietor or set up a marketing function. This book is written to help you achieve your goals.

The only real difference between a successful company and a struggling one is great marketing talent. Most of your competition has not made the connection between marketing and revenue generation. They may see marketing as an unnecessary cost—expenditure versus investment. In reality, the best investment a company can make is to hire quality marketing people. They will generate sales.

But most companies do not have a dedicated marketing function. Small companies assume that marketing is advertising and rely mainly on yellow pages or print ads in various magazines and journals. Yellow pages and most magazines and journals usually don't have successful copywriters working on the ads. Do not work with an advertising agency unless they have a dedicated copywriter working on staff. In general, you'll find marketing is referral-based in 90 percent of small companies without structured, disciplined, or systematic referral systems. All referrals are through chance.

Large corporations, on the other hand, usually have a marketing communications department to focus on in-house designs and trade shows. Plus they have product managers who know everything about the product but perhaps little about how to extract value from it or how to put it in a context useful to others.

Rarely do I find organizations with marketing professionals who understand and apply the concepts I share with you in this book.

Yet without marketing, there is no way to generate sales. A sale is simply the result of effective marketing: showing others the value and helping people make the decision to purchase.

Without a dedicated black belt marketer in your organization, your competition will always be taking business from you. I have helped several companies achieve significant sales growth and return to profitability by using the techniques taught in this book. My desire is for you to take advantage of the benefits and privileges that marketing offers, and make the revenue-generation process successful! To master anything, you must practice daily.

Marketing is the key to the lock. It opens the door to sales. It's a tough lock to open if you have never had exposure to marketing. But there is hope. This book is your marketing reference handbook. Keep this handbook with you and refer to it often!

MOVE

17

Go cable, then go national

MOVE 17

Go cable, then go national

Some people think television advertising is reserved for Fortune 500 companies. This is not true. You can purchase a cable advertising commercial for as little as $10 to $15 per thirty-second commercial. Several hundred thousand people can be reached through your local cable company, just for the price of a cup of coffee a day for a month.

I recently saw my local painter on my area CNN channel. When you view a cable channel, you view it through your city's local provider. This is perfect, because it gives your business the opportunity to test. If the ad pulls a good response, you can scale larger and become wealthy!

Most large corporations will spend millions of dollars advertising on national television. Local cable channels are far more affordable and a smart move for black belt marketers. Build one market at a time, test the effectiveness of the ad, and, when it works, scale up and make millions.

Besides cable TV, you may also want to explore marketing with your local network-affiliated TV station. Reporters and editors, like everyone else, love food. Get to know your local television editors and reporters by inviting them to lunch. Send a note, and position yourself as an expert they can call upon for a quote when a story develops that involves your expertise. An article with a quote written by you brings a lot more credibility than any paid advertisement. If you don't know who covers your industry, observe what reporters write about or call the news desk.

"I saw you on TV." TV advertising elevates your business higher than your competitors. There's something magical about advertising on television that makes people take you more seriously (unless of course your commercial is poorly made or your message is unclear).

Getting your business on television requires a small upfront investment. The initial production of a simple ad can cost approximately $2,000 to $2,500. But once you have made the one-time fixed investment, other expenses are variable. You can also use the produced video elsewhere. It can be used on a satellite station or national TV station that has access to a much larger audience.

Cable TV is perfect for companies selling products directly to consumers. If you currently run yellow page ads and pay $2,500 per month, try cable and track the results. Don't forget that to get a good response, you need both reach and frequency.

Advertising Effectiveness = Reach x Frequency x Quality of Message

Once you reach the right audience with the right message and the right frequency, your product or service sales will explode. The only way to figure it out is through testing. Television is no longer only for big companies. A local painter, accountant, pizza restaurant, or mortgage broker can get on TV. It can be effective and give you instantaneous access to several hundred thousand—or perhaps even a few million—people.

MOVE

18

Master the greatest sales tool in the world

MOVE 18

Master the greatest sales tool in the world

W hat's the greatest sales tool in the world? The telephone! It allows you to connect with anyone in a matter of seconds. The ability to use the telephone effectively is a move you must master to earn your black belt in marketing.

The telephone is the cheapest way to do your marketing. Why does the phone work so well?

- No appointment needed

- Reach a contact in a matter of seconds

- People always listen to voicemail. You can have a progressive conversation.

Whatever business you are in, the telephone can easily give you between a 30 percent and a 500 percent increase in sales. The phone allows you to make value propositions directly to the persons who need to hear them. It provides access to decision makers in the shortest amount of time.

GET YOUR BLACK BELT IN MARKETING

Black belt marketers seize opportunities faster than anyone else. Many others may see the telephone as just another means of communication. But, as a black belt marketer, you see the telephone as a very powerful marketing tool.

A five-minute quality conversation with the right person can change your business life forever.

Many businesses simply pick up the phone and make random calls, but black belt marketers are better prepared. When you call and ask for someone's valuable time, you must make it worth their while by providing quality and valuable information. Never call someone unless you have a script. Before calling a prospect, a black belt marketer should know three things:

1. Why they are calling
2. The value their prospects will gain from them
3. The message written out with the key points highlighted

The black belt marketer must also follow the four Ps of telephone marketing.

- Polite
- Positive
- Professional
- Prepared (have a script)

The key to successful telemarketing is having a script. A script is not definitive; it is directional. It ensures you hit the key points, and it keeps you on target.

People actually welcome telephone calls because it makes them feel important. If you call with valuable information, your prospects will be grateful to you. In sales we help people make decisions, and a telephone call can provide information to help people to do so.

Here are a few more tips on telemarketing:

114

MOVE 18: MASTER THE GREATEST SALES TOOL IN THE WORLD

1. CARE BEFORE YOU CALL.

Before you pick up the phone, your goal must be to help others, not to annoy them! Sales is simply serving, helping people and improving their lives. Call because you care, and this will show in your voice. People can sense your sincerity and motives.

2. HAVE A SCRIPT.

Make sure to have a written script of what you plan to say, and practice it several times. It should be solid in content and value and sound natural. Keep the message simple and short.

"Hello, Peter, this is Ali Pervez. I noticed you've not purchased xyz for the last three months. We currently have a special, and I would like to give you some details. Please call me at 925-786-XXXX. I look forward to hearing from you. Thank you."

3. LISTEN TO YOUR MESSAGE AFTER YOU HAVE RECORDED IT.

If they do not pick up the phone (which will happen perhaps 90 percent of the time), leave a quality message. At the end of your message, always hit the # key. This will allow you to listen to your message, and even rerecord it. After listening, rate your message. On a scale of one to ten, how does it measure in the three Cs?

Clear
Compelling
Crisp

I guarantee you will want to rerecord your message. There is always room for improvement.

4.LOVE VOICEMAIL!

Ninety percent of the time you will reach voicemail. That's great! Your competition will see this as voicemail jail. But black belt marketers are trained to see it as having a progressive dialogue. Everyone listens to voicemail. So the next time you call, which should be after one week, say, "Sorry I missed you," and give your message again. When they do finally pick up the phone, they will likely apologize to you.

5. KEEP CALLING UNTIL THEY PICK UP THE PHONE OR RETURN YOUR CALL.

It is not uncommon to leave up to twelve messages over a period of a few weeks before you either connect or get a call back. Is this pestering or bothering? For black belt marketers, it's a necessary way to add value.

As I explained earlier, you're not out to sell but to improve the lives of others. You can also protect your customers by allowing them to buy from you, because someone else may take advantage of them. Your goal is to make sure they make the right decision: to choose you over someone else.

You are in black belt marketing to change people's lives in a positive way. If you believe this, continue to call until you connect. Your prospects will respect you if they know you care more than the competition.

For an in-depth discussion of telemarketing, refer to *Marketing is King!* (www.blackbeltinmarketing.com).

MOVE
19

Get a database

MOVE 19

Get a database

There are two assets that when leveraged are almost certain to enable your company to succeed in marketing.

- Testimonials from customers
- Referrals from customers

But the question is, who are your customers? Most organizations do not know. The only way to know your customers is through keeping a database.

Most marketers will tell you that if they had everything taken away from them, the one thing they would keep is the database. Some people call this their list. Databases are essential in marketing. Successful companies use databases.

It's only through the database that you know who your customers are. You can ask for testimonials and referrals, develop a long-term relationship, and inform your customers of new opportunities. But, having said this, I am amazed at how few companies actually have a database. These companies just expect customers to turn up on a regular basis.

GET YOUR BLACK BELT IN MARKETING

In early 2000, the famous real estate author Robert Allen said, "Sit me at the keyboard of any computer in the world with access to the Internet. And in 24 hours, I'll earn at least $24,000 cash" (Source: Robert Allen, *Nothing Down*).

On May 24, 2000, he did a live challenge and made $94,532.44 in twenty-four hours. What was the secret? How was he able to do this in such a short period? He had a database of 11,518 current subscribers to his products. Over the twenty-four-hour period, he sent them all e-mails with a great offer. Granted, it had taken several years to create such a database. But here's the point:

Database = Money in Marketing

The database doesn't have to be huge. I have known companies with a database of only three thousand people that sell several hundred thousand dollars per week. Just keep returning to the database.

You don't even need to sell your product; you can offer your database to other people. Your database can simply be a channel for other people's products or services.

You already have a database if you are in business. You have collected business cards. You have a name, a phone number, an e-mail. Are you putting these into a database? Go to a company like CardScan and buy software that automatically scans in your cards. The equipment costs less than two hundred dollars.

They will also allow you to access the information online free. I did this with all my business cards several years ago, and now have about 1,100 business contacts I have accumulated over the years. The service automatically sends out e-mails asking people to update their information; it is a powerful tool.

A database is a list of people with whom you've developed a level of trust. People always listen to and buy from people they know, like, and trust. A golden rule of sales says, "The more you know about

120

your customer, the more interested they will be in you." A database not only helps you store information about your customers, but it also allows you to update it to keep track of what is of value to them.

A sole proprietor can simply use an Excel spreadsheet. Here is an example of how to lay it out:

Name	Address	Telephone	e-mail
Jo Do	4434 Larwin Rd	925-555-xxxx	Jo@aol.com
	Marketville		
	California 94521		

Can you see the impact of having this information readily available? You can now set up regular communication and progressive mailings. This means being in touch on a consistent and regular basis. If there is value in the information you send, it will be welcomed and reviewed. The purpose of sending out information is to allow your customers to choose you over someone else. Help them to make informed decisions.

Don't just put your business card in an envelope. Put them into a database, then send a letter to the people that gave you their business card and explain what is happening in your world. As a business owner, you are considered an expert in your field. People often look to you for advice. A mailing is your opportunity to add value, to show people you care, and to gain respect.

A dry cleaner could write a short article on how to reduce allergies by having clothes dry-cleaned regularly. This is certainly of value to many people in the spring and at other times of the year. At the end of your letter, ask for referrals.

Constant communication with your customers and prospects creates trust and loyalty. Communication first starts with knowing who your customers are. Develop a database in Access, XL, ACT!, or any other database that will track your customers' (or your prospects') information. Keep the database up-to-date.

GET YOUR BLACK BELT IN MARKETING

This sounds obvious, but many companies have no idea who their customers are. They're simply grateful they show up! You are a master black belt, and you not only know your customers, but you know a lot about them. Capture this information in your database.

If you don't have a database, rent one from someone in a similar business or someone already marketing to suitable targets or prospects. Many professional marketers do this. They find a company with a well-maintained database and ask to mail to the list. Be creative. For example, my dentist has a database of two thousand people.

If I gave her a mailing piece introducing my book and offered her 40 percent of the profits, do you think she would be interested? I would immediately get access to two thousand more people! It would take a long time to build that kind of list!

All professional marketers share or rent databases from good sources. The official marketing term is *list rental*. Once you develop your own database, you can also rent your database.

Most Internet marketing courses boil down to one thing: how to develop a database.

It's common sense that you need someone to market your product or service to. The more contacts you have, the more your chances to be successful. I consult for a software company in Silicon Valley. The CEO was going to a trade show, and he asked me how to approach the show. My advice was: "Look at each exhibitor at the show and ask yourself a question: Would you like access to their database?"

Developing a partnership with just a few exhibitors would develop a mailing list of several thousand people! Remember that databases today are all opt-in. This means that people give permission to market (bring value) to them. And once they give permission, it is your responsibility to bring value. You do them a disservice if you do not bring value. This is a basic move, but a move that many businesses overlook. Practice it, and you will generate cash!

MOVE

20

Work your database

MOVE 20

Work your database

Do you want to double your sales in the next year? Then you must work your database to build relationships!

As you learned in the previous move, a database is an asset to any organization. To use it effectively, segment it into types of contacts (suspects, prospects, and customers). Then you can develop an effective strategy for each, depending on where they are in the sales cycle.

Segment your database

Type of contact	Stage in the sales cycle
Suspects	Have some interest in your product.
Prospects	Have interest and money. They want to know why to choose you over anyone else; they need to be educated.
Customers	Have paid and are happy with the performance and result

125

Type of contact	Recommended strategy
Suspects	Send information to help suspects qualify as prospects.
Prospects	Qualify prospects as customers by educating them on the value to be gained from your product or service.
Customers	Focus on obtaining referrals and testimonials and converting them into clients that buy often and refer you to others.

Management of a database is not a trivial task. It takes careful segmentation, and each segment has its own strategy.

For example, if you have existing customers, how many have been with you for one year/five years/ten years? Do they not deserve recognition, much like you would give to an employee of similar tenure? Send them a gift voucher based on their length of tenure with your organization. If you reward them, they will reward you with business for years to come.

Customers can further be segmented into the three Ps of Marketing:

Past customers
Present customers
Potential customers

The communication approach to each group is different. Call, write, and communicate to reactivate past customers. They have purchased from you in the past, and you want them back.

You want present customers to come more often, buy more, and refer more. Make it easy for potential customers to start a buying relationship with you as quickly as possible.

Most organizations don't have a database, and many who do have no idea how to work them effectively. They have never segmented or divided the database into the different types or defined a communication strategy for each.

Advanced black belt marketers do yet another level of segmentation of their customers.

Platinum	People who keep you in business
Gold	People who do good business with you
Silver	People who buy
Bronze	People who buy on/off
Lead	High-maintenance people who hold you back

Segmenting your database into the above five categories will quickly affect your revenue. Drop the lead customers and focus efforts on the platinum and gold ones. Just by doing this, you can easily double your sales.

Out of touch means out of control. Budget the cost of regular mailings into a marketing budget. Well-recognized companies are the ones people see and hear most frequently. If you don't think of your prospects and customers, they won't think of you! Your database is a list of your followers: be a leader. Continually educate customers and help them make informed and intelligent decisions. They will buy more, more often, and refer more to you!

The entire concept of managing a database is one of the higher-level moves of black belt marketing. Your database is central to your success. Back it up and keep all contacts in a safe place. A good contact in the business world means the potential to make money. Use it effectively, and it will make you money.

MOVE
21

Simplify

MOVE 21

Simplify

Black belt marketing ensures people will buy your product or service in the shortest possible time. Marketing is successful only if customers and prospects can immediately see the value offered to them. Today, customers are more overwhelmed and confused than at any other time in marketing history, because they are bombarded with advertisements. It is estimated by most marketing experts that we see anywhere from fifteen thousand to twenty thousand advertisements per day.

Whatever vehicle you choose to communicate your message, your message must be simple and crisp to be effective. Simplicity sells.

You no doubt have heard of the elevator pitch. Try it. Next time you're in an elevator and someone walks in, tell them exactly what you do and how you can help them by the time you reach the sixth floor. And get their business card!

For example, I am in a lift, you walk in, and the conversation goes as follows:

Me: "Hi, how are you?"

You: "Great!"

Me: "What brings you here today?"

You: "Oh, I just need to see my accountant."

Me: "Yeah, I suppose that is important, but if you know how to market effectively the accounting will take care of itself."

You: "What do you mean? What do you do?"

Me: "I'm an author and a marketing specialist, and I believe marketing is for everybody. I help people use marketing in all areas of their life, be it business, personal, or social. It applies to everybody."

You: "Wow, you're a really interesting person."

Me: "No, I'm just different. Here's my card. Give me a call sometime. Can I take yours?"

Notice how I got the message across. It was clear, crisp, and engaging. In the same way, let others quickly see what you have to offer. Marketing is about being simple. The best copywriters write the way most people speak: in plain English. The best ads are the ones that explain the value of products or services in everyday language.

If you want to connect with people, talk their language. Most newspapers are written at an eighth grade level. Don't try to use complex jargon or words to impress your audience. Be real. However complex your product or service, simplify it and make it relevant to your audience. Educate your prospects and customers without sounding like a grammar school teacher!

The more you simplify, the more you sell. People love simplicity; they want things that can save time, money, and stress. Make your products:

- Easy to understand
- Easy to use
- Easy to recommend

I recently brought a roller walker for my elderly mother. The box read "no tools required." The set-up guide was four simple steps, and my nine-year-old son was able to set it up. By making the set-up quick and easy, the company showed it cared about its customers. A toll-free number was also provided.

The software company SAP makes highly sophisticated enterprise software, and one of the major reasons they are successful is that it is easy to use. Strive to simplify your message into three key bullet points such as "easy to install," "easy to use," and "easy to maintain." Never assume any understanding on the part of your customers. The black belt marketer's job is to make other people's lives better and easier.

MOVE

22

Know the secret

MOVE 22

Know the secret

B lack belt marketers master how they use their minds and their marketing skills. One way to do this is by watching the movie *The Secret* at www.thesecret.tv.

The movie (and the book *The Secret* by Rhonda Byrne) shows how we attract what we want in life: spiritually, financially, emotionally. What is the secret? The law of attraction! Like attracts like, similar to a magnet. The thoughts we think, the feelings we feel, the words we say, and the actions we take all consist of energy that attracts more of its own kind. Thoughts become energy that changes life.

In Masaru Emoto's book *The Hidden Messages in Water*, he points out how people in Japan were able to change molecules of water in the Fuji River by their thoughts. Depending on the thoughts, different changes were observed in the shape of water crystals. This is one of the best examples of the law of attraction in action, which is explained in the book *The Secret*.

The key take-away point from *The Secret*: You will move in the direction of your dominant thoughts, and you will become what you think about. Your mind is like a GPS navigation system. Once you program it to a destination, it can't help but take you there.

We create our circumstances and conditions in life through our thoughts. Our thoughts lead to our feelings, and the feelings we hold are sent to the universe. The people in your life do not just show up; you attract them with your thoughts and feelings.

Many businesses focus on why things are not working out. Consequently, their minds are not searching for solutions but proving them right. The Secret shows the key to success is to focus on what we want and to shut off negativity. Focus on the positive, and you will head in that direction.

The Secret teaches us to command from the universe what we want, and it will deliver it to us. Our job is to think daily about what we want, where we want our business to take us, and leave it to the universe to deliver it. Once you start to visualize your path with clarity, like GPS, you will automatically start to follow that path.

Wealth is a mind-set. To become successful in business, you must think as successful people do. Dream and have clear goals. Set your thoughts on business growth, and it will happen.

Black belt marketers know the secret and that written goals become reality. They are your direction in life. Write down your sales target for this year and next year. Study these goals daily. Don't worry about how you will achieve it. That is for the universe to decide. Notice how you automatically start to move in the direction of your dominant thoughts. That's the law. Don't worry about how, just know why. That's what *The Secret* is all about.

Most people think that all goals must be achieved, but this is not true. It is not what the goals do for you, but what they make of you in the process of achieving them. I had a dream to write a book, and I did. But in the process of writing the book, I have become a different person.

Once you fix your mind on what you want and visualize it daily, you cannot help but go there, as long as you believe in your goals with total certainty.

Practice the secret daily.

MOVE

23

Advertise effectively

MOVE 23

Advertise effectively

Here are the biggest complaints I hear from business people:

"My advertising is not working."
"I can't afford advertising."
"I never get any results from my advertising."
"Advertising is a waste of money."

Is it that advertising does not work, or is it that you're going about it the wrong way? Let me share with you another marketing secret.

Words sell, so choose your words wisely.

An advertisement is no more than a collection of words, and perhaps a graphic. Choose your words effectively, and you will get attention.

Advertisements work, but only if they are written by successful marketing professionals. On the next page, you can see an advertisement by Albert D. Lasker in the late 1800s. He is considered one of the founding fathers of marketing. Notice how effective this advertisement is, although it is over a hundred years old! The image gets your immediate

You Hear!
When you use

Wilson's Common Sense **Ear Drums**

The only scientific sound conductors. Invisible, comfortable, efficient. They fit in the ear. Doctors recommend them. Thousands testify to their perfection and to benefit derived.

Information and book of letters from many users, free

WILSON EAR DRUM CO.

103 Trust Building   Louisville, Ky.

Source:

The Story of Albert Lasker.
John Gunther

attention if you are having a problem hearing. The headline identifies the problem and shows you the solution. Then it provides you with the value you can gain by purchasing this product. Finally it shows that there are testimonials to validate the product.

David Ogilvy's 1958 ad for Rolls-Royce remains one of the most famous automobile advertisements of all time. The company was on a particularly tight budget, and Ogilvy was asked to perform the impossible: create an ad that people would never forget. Ogilvy achieved the impossible with one simple sentence: "At sixty miles an hour, the loudest noise in this new Rolls-Royce comes from the electric clock."

This headline helped double that firm's American sales in a year. These are just two examples of advertising done correctly. Choose the right mix of words to create the right emotions and feelings in your audience, and you can sell anything.

Top-notch marketers are trained wordsmiths. We choose the right words to do the selling for us. You saw how this works in move 11, when we talked about the power of the word you. All black belt marketers know that the most important part of an advertisement is the headline. The headline is the first thing someone sees. Top black belt marketers spend days experimenting with words to create irresistible headlines. How about

"How my ten-year-old son makes $1,000 a week on the Internet, part-time."

If you read this headline and you have a boy about that age, you'd want to learn more!

Black belt marketers are masters of using the right words in the right context at the right time. The dictionary can be a powerful tool!

Using words in an effective way leads to effective communication. Here's a simple example. If I want to tell you that you're wrong, I can tell you in many different ways.

"You are mistaken."

"That may be incorrect."

"You are a liar."

Each one creates a different emotion, all with words. What if I told you I could get an avalanche of new customers for you over the next thirty days? Did I get your attention? Of course. But what was the key word? *Avalanche.*

Your choice of words do the selling for you. Vivid pictures create emotions, and all human beings are emotionally driven. Emotions ultimately move people to action. Emotions have even started wars. Marketing is a powerful force, because the way words are used generates feelings. Names of products and companies should be chosen carefully. Names create a feeling, and feelings move people to action.

If I say XYZ is a name you can trust, do I get your attention? Yes, because I used the word *trust,* and that one simple word creates a sense of security within you. Study the ads that have an impact on you, and highlight the key words that make the ad effective. You will notice these words create emotion. Keep a file of ads that make you act. Soon you'll learn how to write a quality ad that relates to your audience by choosing your words correctly.

GET YOUR BLACK BELT IN MARKETING

The purpose of advertising is to sell. It shows people the value they can gain through a purchase. Products or services come into existence to solve problems. Marketing exists to show the market how products and services solve those problems.

Advertising is not just used to create awareness. Creating awareness is just one step in the sales process. Unless your advertising is selling for you, it is not a good investment. Let's look at how advertising works and the steps you should take to get someone to buy your product or service. There are four basic steps to any advertisement.

Steps	Time spent on each
1. Who are you?	90%
2. What do you do?	5%
3. What can you do for me?	4%
4. Why should I buy from you?	1%

Notice that 95 percent of most advertisements' time today is spent on who you are and what you do. Only 5 percent is spent on what you can do for me and why I should buy from you. But these two questions are subconsciously asked by the audience: What can you do for me? Why should I buy from you?

Most advertising tells people what you do. But to capture people's interest, tell them what you can do for them!

To sell a product or service through an advertisement, choose words that clearly show people what you can do for them and why they should buy from you. This is the value proposition. A value proposition has economic value to someone.

Advertising is simply salesmanship in print. Always remember that effective advertising shows the value a product or service can add to another's life. Carefully select the words and pictures you use, and you will begin to master this move.

146

MOVE
24

Master the four moves
to sales checkmate

MOVE 24

Master the four moves to sales checkmate

Whatever the nature of your business, you must master sales. Effective selling skills can be mastered in four moves.

1. IMMEDIATELY SET UP AN IV (INFORMATION AND VALIDATION).

The common misconception most people have about sales is that it is intrusive and forces people to buy what they don't want or need. But black belt marketers know they never really sell; instead, they help people make the right decisions on what to buy. In a selling situation, you are helping a customer. You are a valuable resource. (In the following illustration "Old" is the old way of thinking about marketing. "New" is the new way of thinking about marketing with a black belt mind-set.)

Old

Sell  BLACK BELT MARKETING

New

Help others make
the right decision
Serve others

GET YOUR BLACK BELT IN MARKETING

How can we help a customer make an informed decision? To make an informed decision, the customer needs only two things: information and validation.

People make decisions by first gathering information about the product or service (in either verbal or written form). Then prospects or customers validate the facts through friends or other sources.

The secret to selling is in knowing how people buy. Follow this path:

1. Provide as much fact-based information on the value someone will gain through using the product or service. The more objective, the better. As I pointed out earlier, education is always the best way to sell. You can never overeducate. People always want to learn.

2. Provide as many testimonials as possible to confirm claims and substantiate the benefits.

3. Allow the opportunity to try the product or service risk-free.

The defining moment for a product or service is always the first time customers try it, not when they buy it. They must truly love it the first time they try it.
Whatever the nature of business, salespeople must have the feeling that their job is to help people. Salespeople show the perceived value that the prospect desires. Black belt marketers are out to add positive value and make a valuable contribution to the world.

Remember the more you help, the more you sell. This is accomplished by giving an IV—information and verification. That's the evidence that the product or service works.

MOVE 24: MASTER THE FOUR MOVES TO SALES CHECKMATE

2. UNDERSTAND THAT A SALE IS A PROCESS NOT AN EVENT.

Selling is the ability to help customers reach an informed decision. The first step is to provide information and verification. The next step is to recognize that a sale is a process not an event. Those with no sales training will expect to get a sale on the first meeting or communication. Providing information once does not always get a sale. Selling simply doesn't happen that way.

Sales is a trust-building process. Customers want several interactions before they make a decision to purchase. The higher the value of the transaction, the longer it will take for the transaction to happen. Keep in touch with customers, even after they have bought your product or service. You can continue to educate them to buy and refer more.

Black belt marketers sell all the time. Every letter, phone call, or meeting with a prospective customer is a minor sale. Take care of the details, and the sale will fall into place.

3. FOCUS ON PERCEIVED VALUE TO OVERCOME PRICE OBJECTION.

The biggest objection any salesperson faces is price: how to price products or services and how to handle price objection. Handle price objection by focusing on value. At the end of the day, people buy value, which is reflected in the price they pay. If a customer hesitates on the price, it's a red flag that they don't see the value!

Customers initially see all products and services the same way. Marketing should show customers the additional value offered by your product in comparison to the competition. The market is trained to turn all products and services into commodities. As a marketer, your job is to prove differently. You know the more differentiation in your product or service, the more value is has in the market, and the more people will pay for it.

BMW is not the same as a Toyota Corolla, although they are both made of metal and have tires. BMW is a differentiated car. In the same way, learn to defend your product or service by quickly pointing out the value added. Never assume a customer can figure it out. The magic word is *education*. Take every opportunity to educate your market on the additional value your product or service offers. How much can others benefit from it?

Perceived value = Perceived benefit/Price to attain the benefit

When someone buys a product or service, they have an expectation of the perceived value they expect to gain. This is the x=y, or expectation line, in the graph below.

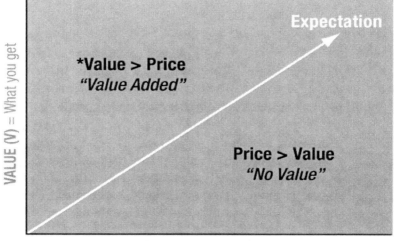

PRICE (P) = What you pay

*A sale occurs when the Perceived Value > Price

Sale = PV > Price

The goal in selling is to show customers more perceived value than they expect for the price they paid. If you do this, you will not have a problem selling. Price won't be an issue.

4. GO ABOUT SALES IN A SYSTEMATIC WAY—FOLLOW THE SIX-STEP PROCESS.

Generating sales is a systematic process.

1. **Generate leads/suspects.** All sales start with a lead. You must have a formal lead-generation method in place, because, without it, sales dry up. The best way to generate leads is through education. Send your market useful information or value items. Give them the IV—information and verification.

2. **Convert leads to prospects.** Prospects are well-qualified leads. To qualify leads, put them through a filter. Ask them a series of questions to determine whether the lead is not only interested but has the money to fit your buying criteria.

3. **Build rapport with prospects.** Build a relationship with a well-qualified prospect. Though most marketers miss this point, people buy from those they know, like, and trust. Relationships are the intangible that make the tangible possible.

4. **Make the value proposition.** Once you have a prospect and have formed a relationship, make the value proposition. Why should they buy from you? Give them reasons why you are the right choice for them, such as the economic benefit.

5. **Handle objections.** However good the offer or value proposition, there will be questions. Have standard scripts ready to handle objections. Objection handling is a predictable part of the sales process.

6. **Get referrals.** Once you've sold the product or service and have a satisfied customer, convert this satisfied customer into a salesperson. You'll never have to cold call again!

Break down the sales process into these six moves, and constantly look at ways to improve each step. If you do this, you will create a revenue-generating business.

MOVE

25

Focus on value not need

25

Focus on value not need

Ninety percent of the marketing texts on the shelves claim that marketing is about finding a need and filing it. As a black belt marketer, you know differently. Marketing is finding out what people want and value and then delivering it.

This is why many companies struggle and spend significant amounts of time and money trying to find out what people need. But when they do, people don't buy it! Why? Although they may need it, they do not value it enough to part with hard-earned cash. We're all told we need to eat five servings of fruits and vegetables a day, to exercise, and not to smoke. But how many of us follow these guidelines?

I have been part of several focus groups over my career. In these groups, people are asked about their views on a proposed product or service. An obvious question is often forgotten in these groups: Would they buy the proposed product or service?

The difference between a need and a want in marketing: a need is something nice to have, whereas a want is a must-have. People get what they want in life, not necessarily what they need.

Need is another word for benefit. But just because something benefits you does not necessarily mean you will buy it. That's why we have the value proposition, not the benefit proposition. People will always pay for what they value; it's the must-have. Once you understand this distinction, you will have a clear advantage over the competition.

Let me provide you with another way to differentiate between need and want. Think of two people arguing about ending a relationship. One person wants the relationship to work, so the last thing he says to the other is: "So what do you really want?"

They don't say, "So what do you really need?" It is past the need stage. It is the absolute, and absolute is always the want or value. This is a small but powerful distinction all black belt marketers know. It's all about customer wants in marketing—the perceived value they desire.

A want is equivalent to a must, and people always get what they must have in life. A need is simply a wish list. As you change your mind-set to think like a true black belt, focus on asking customers or prospects these questions: What do you really want? What is of value to you?

These simple questions help prospects and customers share their expectations, something they will move toward. It's a powerful marketing question because it help you to find what is of value to them. Once you know this, you are in a position to deliver it.

This simple change in the question that you ask will have a profound impact on the way you market.

Let your competition focus on what people need, the wishful thinking. In the meantime, find out what your customers want and value, and guess who wins? Once you recognize what people value, you own the transaction.

MOVE
26

Get a mentor

MOVE 26

Get a mentor

To build marketing muscle, we need to push harder. The best way to challenge yourself is through a coach or mentor. Find someone who will

1. Help set goals

2. Hold you accountable

3. Guide you

4. Give expert advice and support

All successful businesspeople have mentors.

Individual	Mentor
Jack Canfield, co-creator, *Chicken Soup for the Soul*	W. Clement Stone
Robert Kiyosaki, author, *Rich Dad, Poor Dad*	Raymond Aaron

GET YOUR BLACK BELT IN MARKETING

Robert Allen, best-selling author   Jay Abraham

Tony Robbins, motivational speaker   Jim Rohn

Jay Conrad Levinson,   Leo Burnett
"The Father of Guerrilla Marketing"

I have people I go to for advice on a regular basis. We all need support, and our support should come from people who have been where you want to go and from those you respect.

When I talk to college students, my advice is always the same: get a mentor. A mentor can hold you to your word, guide you, and save you lots of time. For example, if you were looking at real estate as a career, how would you like to have Donald Trump as a mentor? Most of us would agree he is a smart real estate investor.

However large or small your business, find a mentor. Call or write someone you respect, and ask them if they are willing to mentor you. Ask them for coaching time; even twenty minutes a week can be very helpful. Believe me, most people are honored that you would even ask.

If you are involved with an organization, it's even easier to find a mentor. Seek out the number one performers in the organization, and ask them if they will help you. Top performers will, because they want the organization to succeed. Your immediate boss should also be your mentor if he or she is a quality manager, because a good boss always trains people to grow into his or her position.

What's in it for mentors? What's the value to them? Where is the marketing element? Most people want to give back to society in some way. The primary reason I wrote this book is to give back, to help as many people as I can with my marketing knowledge. I have mentors I trust and respect in all areas of life, including finance and marketing. Some call it a network, but it is more than that. These people know what works and save me lots of time.

162

The concept of mentoring is a fundamental principle of marketing. It is tested. Your mentor has been where you want to go. If you cannot get a real person as a mentor, read books and listen to CDs and podcasts by people you respect regularly. It's the next best thing.

Highly successful people have enough humility to ask others for help. As long as your goal is to benefit others, there are people out there who have exactly what you want. Approach them and get the advice you need to reach the right destination. And make a promise to your mentor that you will also mentor someone else someday.

MOVE
27

Use the Internet as your market
research department

MOVE 27

Use the Internet as your market research department

Abraham Lincoln once said, "If I had eight hours to chop down a tree, I'd spend six sharpening my axe."

Market research is the tool to sharpen the axe. To become a master marketer, you must think differently than your competition and see what your competition does not see—and faster. Your competition will often miss the wealth of information available for free right in front of them: the Internet! The Internet is one of the marketing professional's most valuable and powerful tools, because it provides valuable information in seconds.

The Internet is the world's biggest reference library.

If marketing is about your ability to add value to customers, then the first question you need to answer is, what do your customers value? What is important to them? Where is the opportunity to add value? Do some fundamental market research.

Market research is a tool to find out where the opportunities exist to add value. Once you know what customers value, you know how to market and what your message needs to be. Then you can educate your customers to make an informed decision.

Today, in a matter of seconds, you can gain all the knowledge you want. Your competitors' Web sites are here, and all the associations, trade magazines, and market reports are online. Allocate a certain portion of the day to browse the Internet. Type in key words or phrases and be as specific as possible. If you are a business owner that sells high-end fashion shoes for ladies, try typing

- Ladies fashion shoe trade shows
- Fashion shoe market analysis
- Trends in ladies fashion shoes
- Suppliers of ladies fashion shoes

Many small business owners wait for the phone to ring or for customers to turn up, while they could be learning about the latest trends in business, what the competitors are doing, and what books are being written on the subject area. Lists of prospects are also free on the Internet. Whatever product you are selling, the buyers for these are also on the Internet. You can simply go to the trade association for your industry, and they will have a list of all the members who are people that will be interested in purchasing what you want. You can go to Dun and Bradstreet, as they have a list of every single company in the United States. You can also go to Info USA; they have databases of all types of consumers.

As a black belt marketer, you are trained to be proactive, to see and seize opportunities. The Internet has the name of every trade association in the world, and the latest trends and developments in your particular product area. It's full of presentations, videos, and articles, and is a black belt marketer's gold mine!

Through the Internet, I "met" the following people:

Gary Halbert
Jay Abraham

MOVE 27: USE THE INTERNET AS YOUR MARKET RESEARCH DEPARTMENT

Clyde Bedell
Jay Conrad Levinson
David Ogilvy
Dan Kennedy
Rosser Reeves
John Caples
Eugene Schwartz
Phil Kotler
Theodore Levitt
Claude Hopkins
Albert Lasker
Yanik Silver

Years ago, when I decided my destiny was to teach marketing, I searched for "marketing gurus" on the Internet, got a name, read an article, and got another name. I signed up for newsletters. Soon, I had a stack of marketing literature. I had my own free marketing library!

Free reports, articles, and e-books can be found on the Internet. Send them to your customers, and they will be grateful. This information is a value item. For example, a dry cleaner can get a huge amount of information on the importance of dry cleaning and how it can reduce allergies. She can use it in a letter or other communication with customers.

The Internet can make you look smart. Take advantage of it!

I am who I am to a high degree because of the Internet, and I continue to read as many marketing articles as possible.

The Internet is your market research department. Information helps you make informed decisions. Providing your customers with relevant, timely, and pertinent information is the key to business. Research using the Internet, and quickly get a handle on what the market values. If you want to know what headlines work, go to Amazon. If you want to see what people are buying, go to eBay, and so forth.

Practice this move regularly. Ask five questions daily that you'd like to know about your business. Type them directly into a search engine, such as Yahoo! or Google. You will be amazed at what you find. Some questions may be:

- Information about your competition. Type in the business that you are in. This gives you a list of all the key players; see who comes up first. Do you know them? Study their Web site, order products from them. They are obviously number one for a reason.

- Type in profitability of XYZ companies. This will tell you how profitable the business that you are in is.

- Type in "How to improve the production of XYZ" (with "XYZ" being whatever type of business you are in). This will give you many articles on how to improve the quality of your product.

- Type in market surveys of XYZ company and read all the surveys that have been done in your particular business area.

I think you are now staring to see the idea.

MOVE

28

Marketing = Investment

MOVE 28

Marketing = Investment

One of the most dangerous traps business owners can fall into is hoping customers will turn up without any spending or investing on their part. Customers do not just show up. It costs money to sell products and to acquire customers. This money is called a marketing budget. (I will show you shortly how to calculate a marketing budget (move 31.) You should allocate a fixed amount of money for marketing.

Most business owners think that by having a good product, customers will magically appear. Business does not work this way. People need to know you exist and then the value you can bring to them.

Unfortunately, in many businesses, the marketing function is ineffective. Marketing dollars do not generate any revenue, or enough revenue to justify the investment. Some see marketing as an unnecessary expense. The common response is, "I don't have the money to market." But what if I said, "Give me one dollar, and I will give you five dollars in two weeks with 100 percent certainty"? Would you go for it? More than likely, you would, right?

Marketing is an investment to generate sales. A business owner may start a business by taking out a loan or borrowing from friends or family. Banks and friends invest in the businesses with the understanding that it will be a good investment. In the same way, when you invest in a marketing program, it as an investment in generating sales from customers.

Old View of Marketing   **New View of Marketing**

Spending   ⟹   *Investing*

Customers do not just show up. You must invest to get people to buy.

Successful organizations are no different from yours. They've just made the right marketing investments, and know, with a high degree of confidence, that the investment will generate sales. Marketing is an investment. It's no different from stocks, bonds, or real estate. It's an investment to generate sales.

Business owners who claim they've not generated sales from their marketing efforts have been burned by spending money on a marketing campaign. But that doesn't mean that all marketing is ineffective. They've just made poor investments. Why is it that some of America's top companies have done well for over a hundred years with consistent profit and sales growth? They have made the right marketing investments. Large corporations may seem to waste money on big institutional ads, but they also have an effective sales force. You may see only the part of marketing that does not work. Companies market at different levels. They do press releases, attend trade shows, and sponsor talks. Usually, one of these revenue-generating vehicles pulls in the majority of revenue.

Few people know what works in marketing. In most cases, it boils down to the 80/20 rule: 20 percent of the effort generates 80 percent of the revenue. However, few people can define the 20 percent. The only way to know for sure if a marketing activity is producing sales revenue is to test it.

MOVE 28: MARKETING = INVESTMENT

Why is it so difficult to make the right marketing investment? There are literally thousands of ways to get your message to a target audience. Here are some of them:
- Run ads
  - On radio
  - On television
  - In print in thousands of magazines and newspapers
  - On thousands of billboards across the country
  - On shopping carts
- Use posters/flyers, blogs, business cards, etc.

Which medium will work for you? You won't know until you test. Marketing is not about spending $75,000 to have your product show up on billboards, taxis, or buses, unless you have tested the idea and know with 100 percent certainty that it will generate sales revenue in the short-term or create brand recognition to generate sales in the long-term.

An established business will spend money for marketing out of current sales revenue and use it to generate more revenue. Once you see marketing as an investment, you will actually enjoy spending money because you know you're not actually spending, but investing to make more money. You can't make money unless you invest correctly. Even if you win the jackpot, you still had to invest in the lottery ticket!

So how do you make a good investment?

1. Get all the facts.
2. Be objective.
3. Ask a lot of questions.
4. Run the numbers.
5. Make the numbers a reality!

Savvy investors have the ability to get all the facts and numbers, and then make an objective decision. Approach marketing investing the way a stockbroker does: get the reports, study the facts, look at options and alternatives, and make a decision. Top managers in large organizations are no more than investment bankers. They invest in companies, products, and technologies.

Seeing marketing as an investment is one of the most powerful moves I can share with you. If your sales are going down, the best way to lift them is by making the right marketing investment. Marketing makes people aware that you have something that can bring value to them.

Anthony Robbins became famous by running infomercials. One of his infomercials ran every thirty minutes, twenty-four hours a day somewhere in North America for ten years. Was this a good investment? Sure, as it resulted in selling some thirty million copies of the *Personal Power II* series, worth millions of dollars in sales. He could have easily used other marketing or revenue-generating vehicles, but this one was tested and proven an excellent investment.

A retailer may invest in a great sign. A repair person may get an excellent referral. A manufacturer may run an effective advertisement. In any case, customers do not just show up—something you do makes them come. Invest the time, money, and effort to get them.

We are trained to think of investing from a financial perspective, but investing applies to all areas of our lives. On a daily basis, we invest time, money, and effort into different activities. So examine what marketing investments work and amplify them.

Unfortunately, few businesses these days see marketing as an investment. Yet marketing only has one role in the business world, and that is to generate sales.

MOVE
29

Know that there are only three ways to grow sales

MOVE **29**

Know that there are only three ways to grow sales

Most business owners think there is only one way to grow sales: to bring in more customers. But if you always run around trying to get new customers, you run a promotion, not a business!

Build a successful business by getting customers not only to buy, but to buy more, and to buy more often. It goes back to the basic sales equation:

Sales Revenue = Units × Price × Frequency
Buy **Buy More** **Buy More Often**

1. BUY

Get people to buy by giving them the opportunity to try.

The best way to start a relationship with prospective customers is to have them try your product or service with no risk, obligation, or commitment. This gets the buying relationship started quickly and painlessly.

The easier you make it to try, the more they will buy.

Try before you buy has become standard practice in the United States. A money-back guarantee is no more than the opportunity to try risk-free. If you are confident that you offer truly adds value, allow the customer the opportunity to try it risk-free, with no strings attached.

Business magazines and book clubs use this strategy, estimating that if they get the right people to try, at least 75 percent of them will buy. They understand the numbers. They have tested it and know giving out free products is a good investment. Even at breakeven or a slight loss, they make money over time.

You can easily double sales by lowering the barrier to start a relationship with you. It goes back to the issue of trust: give people the opportunity to trust you. If you truly have a great product or service, give as many people as possible the opportunity to try it risk-free. Some may take advantage, but the majority will turn into loyal customers and clients.

2. BUY MORE

The value meal is a true marketing concept: to show value! If you buy in larger amounts, you get it cheaper. People buy more when they are shown the savings of buying larger quantities versus individual units. There is always the opportunity to sell additional items to customers. Typical examples are extended warranties offered with a car sale, or chips and drinks offered with a Subway sandwich.

If a customer wants to buy paint from a paint store, the owner should have a list of items that complement the sale. Here are some examples:

- Brushes
- Rollers
- Drop cloths
- Masking tape
- Painters caps
- Cleaning supplies
- Ladders

MOVE 29: KNOW THAT THERE ARE ONLY THREE WAYS TO GROW SALES

Does offering these items to customers take advantage of them or help them? It's called up-selling in the marketing world. An up-sell is a benefit for your customers. It saves them money by preventing them from having to go elsewhere to buy supplies, so they will buy more, refer more, and come back more often.

Your goal is to ensure your customers have everything they need to be successful, because if they are successful, you will acquire repeat business and referrals. On average, one out of every three people will buy more if offered an additional or complementary item at the time of sale. Up-selling is easy if you do it for the benefit of the customer.

The key word is *discipline*. Subway is a good example. Counter clerks are trained to ask customers if they would like drinks and chips with their sandwiches. How many times do you attempt to up-sell?
A supplier of blood glucose meters for diabetic patients will ship a catalogue of diabetic supplies with an order. This way, they are seen as a one-stop trusted supplier. The mind-set is to provide everything your customer wants and values and to make their lives easier.

3. BUY MORE OFTEN

If you have a product that can be used repeatedly, you owe it to your customers to "program them" to do business with you. If they do not buy from you, they will buy from someone else. If you run a hair salon and a customer comes in to get his hair cut, you do him an injustice if you allow him to leave without making another appointment. If you really care about how your customer looks and want him to always look his best, you will set his next appointment before he leaves. In fact, you may set a whole year of appointments for him!

By having your customer come back six times a year instead of two, you not only triple your sales but do your customer a huge favor. You have taken care of a huge problem (looking good) in his life.

GET YOUR BLACK BELT IN MARKETING

When you get an oil change, the attendant gives you a sticker to remind you when you need the next one. A carpet cleaner or dry cleaner may give you a refrigerator magnet to remind you to call. It's called programming. Tell customers the exact date and time they should call, and they will! People look for leaders to provide services or products for their benefit. These leaders are black belt marketers. If you say to customers as they leave the premises, "Please come back," they probably will! Schedule them to come back, and they will thank you.

Is this manipulation? No, it's good marketing, and it helps others. Remember the difference between manipulation and marketing is always intention. If I truly want you to look good for your sake, I am marketing. If I just want you to come back six more times during the year to make more money from you, that is manipulation. Black belt marketing is about adding positive value, not taking advantage of people. Frequent flyer programs and loyalty programs are both simple examples of programming.

MOVE

30

Become a master networker

MOVE 30

Become a master networker

I hate networking. The only thing I like about it is that it works, and it works beautifully. Networking is the move of moves for your black belt. You can use it to eliminate your competition. It is a power move. You cannot earn your black belt in marketing unless you master how to network effectively. Networking is used by all master marketers.

Networking is your shortcut to getting things done. If you learn how to network, you become a master of leverage and are able to accomplish a lot with a minimal amount of time, effort, and money.

Master networking, and you will never make a cold sales call again. You then make "warm" calls to people you've been introduced to. They are waiting to hear from you.

All small- and medium-sized businesses are built on referrals, which is a form of networking. All top-performing brokers in the insurance or mortgage industry will inevitably be part of a local networking group. This is the way they become known in their communities.

Why does networking work? Because of the magic word in marketing—*trust* (move 4).

GET YOUR BLACK BELT IN MARKETING

People buy from people they know, like, and trust.

My book *Marketing is King!* was picked up by a major New York publishing house because it was recommended by one of America's most famous marketing gurus. My publisher trusted his recommendation. I was successfully able to network. If you want to learn how to effectively network, I have a full section in the book on the exact process to do it.

To grow a business, you must become a master networker. Make it a habit to collect business cards from every person you meet, and put the cards into a database. A company called CardScan offers a phenomenal free service that allows you to hold all your business cards online. This list can be used to generate subsequent mailings.

A good networking tool I know and use myself is LinkedIn. Set up a profile, and this site links you to people who have worked in the companies you have. You can thus gain access to their network. One person I know knows eighty people, and I can access these eighty people through him. LinkedIn is the underground networking tool. Get in contact with others through your friends.

People move in networks. Everyone has a network. It is a fact that you mix with people who are like you. Jim Rohn, America's foremost business philosopher, says, "You are the average of the five people that you surround yourself with on a daily basis." Your life is a result of your thoughts, and your thoughts are generated by your network. If you want to take your business or your life to a higher level, hang around people who are going places or are where you want to go!

Here are six simple rules of networking:

- Be proactive. Go out and network. People will not come to you.

- Make it a habit to collect business cards.

- Build a relationship with everyone you meet. (Send them a value item on a regular basis.)

- Get permission to access the network of the person that you are going to build a relationship with.

- Always ask yourself, "I wonder where this person can you take me?"

- Keep networking!

Networking is a skill that will change your marketing quickly. Never abuse or misuse this skill, repay your network contacts, and they will always want to help you. And remember, your network determines your net worth!

Know how to calculate a
marketing budget

31

Know how to calculate a marketing budget

H ow much should you spend on marketing? Before I show you how black belt marketers calculate a marking budget, let's study how it is often done today.

Small companies usually have no marketing budget and rely solely on existing customers for repeat business and referrals. Most of them do not have a formal referral system, so referrals are by chance. They happen sporadically. Location and signage is a major revenue generator. If these businesses have any leftover money, they may do a mailing. If an advertising agency makes them an offer, they may take advantage of it. They forget that most people who sell advertising space have little interest in making you money or making you successful.

For most small companies, there is no plan, strategy, or formalized marketing budget. These businesses believe revenue generation is uncontrollable. Customers just turn up. Most of their time is spent developing or making the product or service, with little or no attention to marketing.

Most small businesses operate in a reactionary mode. They have no idea why customers buy, but are happy they do! Customer traffic is similar to the weather; sometimes it's sunny, and other days it rains. Sales are highly unpredictable. Ask these businesses what they can do to improve sales, and they may say, "There is nothing we can do. It's the economy."

Most small companies have spent money on marketing in the past and found no return, so why should they bother? They have not yet been introduced to the world of black belt marketing.

Medium-sized companies usually have a budget set by the person in charge of marketing. The marketing director is told the sales target, and he guesses what marketing expenditure is required to hit the sales goal. The budget is mainly focused on the cost to acquire new customers. Usually, little thought goes into making the marketing budget. To arrive at the budget, these companies may take last year's budget and multiply it by the sales growth desired.

Most medium-size companies will allocate a fixed amount of funds, and the marketing director works within these to develop marketing programs. He will use historic figures to determine how to allocate the funds to different programs. What lift did the company receive in doing certain activities, and what sales were generated? This marketing system is a notch higher than the small business owner's system.

Large companies usually allocate a percentage of sales to SG&A (sales, general and administration). This amount is usually based on what the competition is doing. Financial reports are studied. SG&A can be up to 30 percent of the sales revenue. This means that these large companies are prepared to spend thirty cents of every dollar in revenue to get the sale. They know marketing is important. Most of the folks who run large corporate marketing departments are MBAs who have made the connection between marketing and sales.

Unfortunately, marketing is not mentioned in SG&A annual reports. They just call it selling, general and administration. It should be called MG&A, or marketing, general and administration. The conventional SG&A includes the company's marketing budget. But most large companies cannot breakdown the marketing budget into maintaining customers versus acquiring new ones. Thus, it's ignored all together and called SG&A.

Let us now look at two ways a black belt marketer may develop a marketing budget.

1. USING A COST BASED MARKETING APPROACH

Now that we have seen the reality of the situation, let's move to how a black belt marketer develops a marketing budget. Let's study an example to see how it works. Let's say you sell windows, and your windows sell for $10,000 each. What is the cost to acquire a new customer? We need to look at the sales activities required to sell the windows, break them down, and then cost them all out. This is a relatively simple exercise. It's what manufacturing people call activity-based costing and is often used to calculate the cost of a product.

To acquire a new customer, let's say it takes

- Seven phone calls
- Three customer visits
- Six mailings
- Some advertising
- Some entertainment and gifts

But how much did all this activity cost?

GET YOUR BLACK BELT IN MARKETING

An example of how to calculate "CANC"
Cost to acquire a new customer
Using a cost based marketing approach

Activity	Cost Per Customer
Seven phone calls	$21
One man hour on the phone @ a rate of $60/hr	$60
Three customer visits - Total Ten Man Hours. At $60/hr	$600
Travel expenses for customer visits	$2,000
Cost of sales materials given to customer	$3
Mailing cost of sales materials . Six mailings at $1 each	$6
Allocated cost of print advertising. $10,000 to reach 1,000 people	$10
Entertainment / Relationship	$125
CANC or total cost to acquire a new customer	**$2,825**

If this results in a sale of $10,000, then this means, that

" You need to invest $2,825 to generate sales of $10,000"
" Your marketing costs are 28% of the sales revenue"

If you consistently are generating $10,000 of sales for every $2,825 invested, then you can buy customers all day long.

To get a complete picture, the overall marketing budget must also include the cost to maintain existing customers: So the total marketing budget equals

The cost to acquire new customers   "CANC"
+
The cost to maintain existing customers   "CTM"

In large organizations, the marketing budget is often 75 percent focused on acquiring new customers. In small organizations, 75 percent is often used to maintain existing customers. An effective marketing budget will encompass both. Here are the four steps black belt marketers use to calculate a marketing budget.

1.   Calculate the Units required to achieve your sales goals

Units = Sales Target / Average sales size

2.   Calculate "CANC" (Cost to Acquire a New Customer)

3.   Calculate cost to achieve sales target

194

MOVE 31: KNOW HOW TO CALCULATE A MARKETING BUDGET

Cost to achieve sales goal = CANC x Units to achieve sales goal

4. Add "CTM" Cost to retain customer to this.

Marketing Budget = CANC + CTM
Marketing Budget = Cost to acquire customers + Cost to maintain new customers

In simple terms, set your sales goal or target. Divide this by the average sale size or average size of the transaction. This tells you how many units you need to sell to achieve your target. Multiply this by the cost to sell each unit and then add to this the cost to maintain your existing customer base.

It may seem complex, but if you study it, you'll find it is common sense. And here again you see the power of simplicity and logic.

If you want to get highly scientific, you can also calculate the CTM (cost to maintain your existing customer base) with a high degree of scientific accuracy by the same cost-based marketing approach. How much money did you spend on average to maintain customers? The CTM would also include any technical support costs and capture all marketing costs required to retain a customer.

The point is that you can and should cost out exactly how much is spent to retain and acquire new customers. By doing the math, your marketing budget will becomes effective. Calculating a marketing budget is not an easy move to master, but unless you run the numbers, you are not making fact-based decisions. If you were to calculate your marketing budget using the above methodology, then take it to your finance department of your company or your bank, they would respect you for giving your marketing budget some serious thought and attention.

The more detailed the cost analysis, the more precise your marketing budget will be. Do the calculations above, and you will likely find you are undercapitalizing your marketing. Most companies cut marketing budgets when sales slow down. The irony of the situation is that they usually have no idea how much it costs to get a sale.

Most small businesses and start-ups fail because they never run the numbers. These businesses don't know precisely how much it costs to acquire or retain a customer. Unless you are able to get and keep customers, you will go out of business!

Calculating a marketing budget is of the most important lessons you can learn as a black belt marketer. Run the numbers. Determine how much it costs to get a sale and keep a customer. Use these numbers to determine the marketing budget.

Now you have a basis to go to the bank and ask for a marketing loan. Tell your banker, business partner, investor, or CEO what your marketing budget needs to be to achieve the sales target you want. This is the same process that is used when starting a business. You must calculate what the investment should be.

Effective marketing is about investing money to get people to buy your product or service, and knowing how much it costs to do it.

2. Use LTP

Another way to calculate a marketing budget is to determine the lifetime profitability of a customer (LTP). To determine LTP, look at the total profit generated from a customer over the lifetime of doing business with you. For example, let's say you are a dentist charging $100 per visit. You know each new patient typically comes three times a year for three years. That patient is actually worth $900 in total revenue, not $100. Let's say you make a 40 percent profit. So you have made $360 in profits from this one patient over his or her lifetime. That means you could invest up to a maximum of $360 per customer on your marketing right now to acquire this patient.

MOVE 31: KNOW HOW TO CALCULATE A MARKETING BUDGET

LTP takes a long-range view of what customers are truly worth to you and allows you to make marketing investment decisions based on that worth. Most businesses under-capitalize their marketing, but armed with CANC, CTM and LTP, that should never happen to you! You are a black belt, and your moves should be well thought out.

MOVE
32

Know the three types
of customers

MOVE 32

Know the three types of customers

Most people think there is only one customer: the person who buys from them. The focus remains on that customer and the hope that he or she will continue to buy and to refer others. I believe that most businesses in America do not do any marketing and are quite content with their current customer base. They do not want to invest in acquiring new customers because of previously making the wrong investments in marketing.

There are actually three types of customers, known as the 3P's of marketing.

Present
Past
Potential

Why is this so important? Black belt marketers use a different strategy for each.

GET YOUR BLACK BELT IN MARKETING

Customer type	Strategy
Present	Get repeat business, get referrals and testimonials
Past	Reactivate, call, and get them to do business with you again
Potential	Make the right investment in marketing programs to get them to buy

This incredibly short move should make a black belt marketer stop and think. Customers come in three types. It is essential for your database to be divided into these three types of people, so you can develop effective marketing programs for each.

Let food sell for you

MOVE 33

Let food sell for you

The biggest challenge for salespeople is getting face time with prospects and customers. People are busy. However busy people are, they do need to eat, and this is something black belt marketers leverage.

Nearly all the major pharmaceutical companies take breakfasts, snacks, or lunches to doctors' offices. Many companies do lunch and learns, hold seminars, and offer a free dinner to qualified prospects. A breakfast may cost a few hundred dollars for a small group. Is it a good investment? Yes, if you can get quality time with key decision makers.

One of the number one salespeople in a pharmaceutical company I worked for did more breakfasts in doctors' offices than anyone else. It helped her build relationships and trust, and consequently her sales exploded.

Remember, people like to do business with people they know, like, and trust.

Think again if you believe there is no such thing as a free lunch. Black belt marketers are generous, and, when they offer meals, they get to enjoy quality time with customers and prospects. No matter the type of business, there is opportunity for you to make food part of your marketing strategy.

I can easily get a room full of students for a university talk if I offer free pizza and sodas. It's a great investment if I get the undivided attention of my target audience.

I have literally seen people line up to get food at major scientific conferences when one of the sponsors offers dinner. This strategy will work even better when you ask in advance what type of food people prefer.

Why does food sell so well? Food is not just a prospect attraction strategy. It puts the principle of reciprocity into action. As human beings, we feel the need to repay people for things they give us. Provide food, and people will give you the opportunity to educate them on your product or service. It's a fair trade. Black belt marketers know that food is the way to their customers' hearts and minds. It shows customers that you want to make doing business a pleasurable experience.

MOVE

34

Focus on up-and-coming customers

MOVE 34

Focus on up-and-coming customers

Black belt marketers look for up-and-coming customers. Imagine if you had been a vendor to Microsoft or Apple in the early years—you would be wealthy today! Those vendors who did know exactly what I mean.

Where your customers are today is irrelevant; your concern should be where they will be five years from now. This is another form of networking: sticking close to winners.

I have seen top sales performers go from nothing to number one in the region, just by building solid relationships with small prospects who grew into major players. These sales performers seized opportunities, and their prospects never forgot how these marketers helped them out in tough times.

Examine your database for up-and-coming customers. Who do you want to develop a closer relationship with? Indentify them, and start now. You will find approximately 80 percent of your business comes from 20 percent of your customer base. Focus on this top 20 percent and spend your time, effort, and resources with these accounts, because they offer the greatest opportunity for growth.

GET YOUR BLACK BELT IN MARKETING

Organizations I have worked for have achieved significant sales growth by focusing their efforts on the top twenty accounts and giving them special incentives and bonuses.

This move is universal. It doesn't matter what type of business you are in; all businesses start small, and some grow quite large.

MOVE
35

Use TLC

MOVE

35

Use TLC

We have talked about the power of communication and how marketing communicates the value that customers want. This value can be communicated in different ways. From my own experience, I can tell you that the two most powerful forms of communication are letter and telephone.

Irrespective of the type, size, and nature of your business, you most probably use letters and the telephone to communicate with your market. But a black belt marketer knows that when a letter is combined with a follow-up telephone call, significant impact will be reached.

A black belt marketer will never send out a letter unless there is a follow-up telephone call to go behind it, and ideally before it.

Everyone loves a little TLC! (TLC = Telephone and Letter Combined)

When you combine a telephone call with a letter, you have a powerful form of communication. If I phone to say I will send more information, then, after sending information, follow up with a call to see if you have received it, my chances of success will increase. Quality calls and well-written letters yield high results.

GET YOUR BLACK BELT IN MARKETING

Many struggling business owners do not provide TLC to prospects and customers. When was the last time you sent a letter? When was the last time you called? Many business owners do little communication with prospects and customers.

Direct mail and telephone combinations work better than Internet marketing because the approach is much more direct. Combining a telephone call with a letter allows your value proposition to target a precise prospect.

View the telephone and mail as partners. They must work together, or they will not work at all.

Most mailing programs fail because there is little (if any) follow-up behind the mailings. Don't just call people, and don't just mail them. Unless you do both, these powerful forces cannot have full impact. If you do not follow up with a call after the mailing, you have wasted the cost of your mailing. It's all about TLC—telephone and letter combined.

MOVE

36

Remember that two-thirds of
the money is on the back-end

Remember that two-thirds of the money is on the back-end

As you continue to master the moves to become a black belt marketer, you must learn that a successful business makes money on the back-end not the front-end. Let me give you some examples:

	Front-End	**Back-End**
Pharmaceutical companies	Samples	Repeat prescriptions
Cellular phone companies	Free phone	Monthly phone bills
Satellite dish panies	Free dish	Monthly subscriptioncom-
Printer companies	Free printer	Ink
Books/ magazines	Free trial offer	Monthly subscriptions
Software companies	Free software	Maintenance contracts

GET YOUR BLACK BELT IN MARKETING

In the world of black belt marketing, the real money is made on the back-end. A successful business is built when a customer stays over time and provides residual revenue. A one-time sale is only a promotion. Real money is made when a customer comes back time and time again.

Many people joke that a top salesperson can sell snow to an Eskimo. This is not a sale; it's a promotion. It's only when you can get that Eskimo to buy repeatedly that you begin to make money!

In the examples above, the front-end is the preview to a long-term relationship. Wealth lies in the long-term relationship. A long-term relationship provides the opportunity to have a customer for life. The way to understand how the wealth lies on the back-end is to understand the basic sales formula.

Sales Revenue =	Units ×	Price	×	Frequency
	Buy	**Buy More**		**Buy More Often**
1 =	1/3	1/3		1/3
	2/3	Back-end (Buy More, Buy More Often)		

If you study the formula above, and assume a 1:1:1 relationship, you will notice that two thirds (or about 66.6 percent) of the revenue of any sale is on the back-end. Unless you get customers to buy more and to buy often, you lose two thirds of the revenue potential.

Here is a simple example. You sell one apple at $1 and once per week.

$$\text{Sales Revenue} = \text{Units x Price x Frequency} = 1 \times 1 \times 1 = \$1$$

In another case, you sell one apple at $1 and one pear at $1 to the same customer, twice in a week.

218

MOVE 36: REMEMBER THAT 2/3RDS OF THE MONEY IS ON THE BACK-END

Sales Revenue = Units x Price x Frequency = 1 x 2 x 2 = $4

You had a 400 percent increase in sales by doubling the size of the transaction and frequency to the same customer.

Black belt marketers know that the quickest way to increase revenue is to increase the size and frequency of the transaction with the same customer, versus trying to get new customers. Getting new customers is an expensive venture that only organizations with deep pockets can afford. Plus it is not effective, as two thirds of the sales revenue is on the back-end.

This is the same reason that television infomercials put you on a mailing list and offer complementary products when you call in.

Black belt marketers sell as much or more on the back-end as they do on the front-end. Most marketers make their money this way. Offer customers the opportunity to buy more once they have purchased the base product, and program them to buy frequently with some form of loyalty program. By programming customers to come back on a regular basis, you can actually save them money in the long term. A car repair shop would book you for a regular oil change in advance, as they know that you need to have your car oil changed. If you do not, you will eventually have to pay for it with an expensive service in the long run.

Your back-end is the ability to sell complementary products or services to customers. The back-end should at least be equivalent (if not higher) to the initial sales volume. Never miss the back-end. This is where the wealth in marketing lies.

MOVE
37

Make the most of trade shows

37

Make the most of trade shows

Medium- to small-size businesses often go to trade shows, places where buyers and sellers meet. Even a small company should consider attending trade shows. You don't even have to exhibit, simply network with key people. Thousands of trade shows cover all areas of business annually. Trade shows are a great way to find out what is going on in your market, meet new people, and build business relationships. If you plan to participate in a trade show:

- Be selective on which ones to attend
- Prepare in advance
- Work the show correctly
- Have an aggressive follow-up plan

What I find amazing is that so many companies go to trade shows to collect leads but have little or no follow-up plan after the show. I have seen many organizations in which salespeople do not even follow up on the leads generated! What a waste of effort!

If you do go to a trade show, remember what happens after the event is more important than the event itself. Your ability to follow up, follow through, and close is critical to the success of the show. The best analogy I can give is being set up for a penalty in a soccer game, then deciding not to shoot! It sounds silly, but 90 percent of companies at trade shows focus only on the front-end.

All the wealth in marketing is on the back-end.

The ability to follow up and follow through with leads is essential to getting the sale. Have a progressive follow-up plan after the show. Prepare a series of letters to go out to all leads captured in your database in a sequential and progressive manner. Here is an example of what to do after the show:

After two weeks: Send a thank you letter.

After four weeks: Send a personalized letter stating how your offering can solve your leads' problems, using specific examples. The more specific and customized your communication, the more value is added.

After six weeks: Make a follow-up phone call.

After eight weeks: Have a meeting and presentation.

After ten weeks: Close the sale and get referrals!

If you currently attend trade shows, do you use a follow-up plan? It's not what happens *during* the show but what happens *after* the show that determines the success of the show.

Marketing is a perpetual process: The goal of marketing is to make the experience last longer.

If prospects approach your booth at a trade show and ask for more information, they have a genuine interest in what you have to offer. They have the hope that you can help them make informed decisions. It is your responsibility to complete the obligation. Install a system with a defined path to closure of the sale. Once you set up a progressive follow-up process, you will be in control of the sales process.

Spend thirty minutes a day
with yourself

MOVE 38

Spend thirty minutes a day with yourself

We all have 168 hours in a week, and we all have the same opportunities. Black belt marketers just use their time more wisely and are able to seize opportunities.

No one on this planet has more or less time than anyone else. We all have 168 hours in a week, so the only difference is in how we prioritize the time. Successful people use their time more effectively.

Black belt marketers keep the main thing (what they should be doing, and what can make them productive) the main thing they do on a daily basis.

In *E-Myth*, Michael Gerber points out that the majority of small business owners work "in the business, not on the business." The point Gerber makes is that most business owners are consumed with putting out fires, doing the day-to-day operational things required to keep the business running. But doing the same thing daily will always lead to the same results. The only way to change your results is to take a new action. The only way to grow a business is to stop and ask hard questions. "What will I focus on today?" "Am I in control or being controlled?" "What five things can I do to grow sales?" is another good question. Focus is the ability to see clearly, and black belt marketers take time to do this.

227

Focus is also "Follow One Course Until Successful."

Set the first thirty minutes of every day for yourself. Write down daily sales growth targets for your department, division, or company. Have written goals and review them daily, ideally once in the morning and once before you go home for the day. Goals are your navigation. They tell you what you need to be doing. Goals give you clarity. Your goals show where you need to go. If you don't have goals and don't review them, others will set goals for you and manage your time and your life.

Don't work toward goals; work backward from them. Once you have set goals, work backward from them. Let's say you want your business to make a million dollars in sales next year. Approach it as follows:

Annual Sales Goal	$1 million
Monthly sales target to achieve goal	$83,333
Number of customers required to hit your target of $83,333 in sales per month (based on an average transaction size of about $100)	833
Number of prospects required to get 833 customers per month (at an 80 percent close ratio)	1,042
Number of suspects required to get 1,042 prospects per month (at an 80 percent conversion ratio)	1,302

Based on the math above, you now know that you need to be talking with 1,302 suspects per month, to realistically achieve your sales target of $83,333 per month or $1 million per year. And from this you will determine your activity level that you need to make this happen. Top-flight sales trainers call this "knowing your numbers."

Now you know how to hit your sales goal of $1 million.

MOVE 38: SPEND THIRTY MINUTES A DAY WITH YOURSELF

Here you see how to break down your goals systematically and logically. You can work back from your goal to figure out what to do today to achieve your goal.

To be a black belt marketer, you must learn to manage your time effectively.

MOVE

39

Make the most of your sales materials

39

Make the most of your sales materials

In marketing you produce various sales tools, literature, and promotional items. You give these to educate prospects and customers and also show gratitude. These materials help you to develop loyalty and to get referrals. These items cost money, and some of the items may even be expensive. Some of these materials are probably even lying around collecting dust.

Make the most of every opportunity, action, and event. You produced these items as sales tools. But do you use them all? Marketing is only effective when it produces results and when you get a return on investment from it. That means you should send or give out the materials you've produced. Don't just let them take up space and gather dust in your warehouse or office.

Let me give you an example. The CEO of a Silicon Valley company for which I consult had exquisite $250 custom-made pens. He kept these in his top drawer, but only gave them to a handful of customers. When I asked him why, he said he could not afford to give away pens.

I told him to look at each marketing expenditure as an investment (move 28). Giving an expensive gift to the right person could open doors that had been closed. I told him to make a list of the top customers and of people in those companies that he would like to build a relationship with. I then told him to send each a hand-written note and a pen. I also suggested he call key journalists and writers, ask them to lunch, and give them a pen as thanks for their time. He leveraged the asset (the pen) and gave out the promotional literature we had developed. The result of this was that he developed quality relationships with people that now were more than willing to help him.

The point is that having literature and gifts in your office does you no good. It is better to have these materials out in circulation, bettering the chance that someone will read it, refer it, or act on it!

This is a simple move and a reminder that the mind of a black belt marketer is always looking for the opportunity to add value to others' lives.

MOVE

40

Use AIDA when communicating

MOVE 40

Use AIDA when communicating

Marketers communicate with the market, prospects, customers, and clients through phone, e-mail, or in person. Black belt marketers know AIDA as a well-understood protocol for communicating.

A Attention
I Interest
D Desire
A Action

ATTENTION

The first thing to do in any marketing communication is to get your prospects ' attention. Notice that most television ads start with an attention grabber: Do you have back pain? Do you have trouble sleeping at night? The attention grabber is the headline. A powerful headline is like grabbing someone by the collar and saying, "This is something you need to know."

Here's an example of a powerful headline: "How my 10-year-old son makes $1,000 a week with his own business."

GET YOUR BLACK BELT IN MARKETING

This headline creates enough curiosity to get people to read the rest of the copy. All marketing communication should start by getting you engaged first, and using powerful headlines is an effective way to attract attention.

INTEREST

Once you have their attention, grow interest in what you have to offer. Share specific examples of the types of problems you can solve. Testimonials are one of the best ways to attract people's interests, especially ones that show how others have obtained positive results by using what you have to offer. Connect and relate to the audience at a deeper level. Intimacy is said to be no more than a shared feeling of reality. So share real-world problems. Explain to them how they will be making the right decision.

DESIRE

The next step is to create the desire to purchase the product. How? Show the solution. "Introducing the new XYZ ..." This is the solution to the problem.

ACTION

Now the audience is engaged, interested, and has a desire to purchase. Encourage the viewer to take action. Offer an incentive to move the customer to action. It could be a time-sensitive offer or a bonus gift.

This well-proven protocol is used by top marketing professionals to communicate with prospects or customers. Now you know why infomercials are so successful!

As a black belt marketer, AIDA should be used in any form of marketing communication:

- E-mail
- Letters
- Telephone
- Print ads

MOVE 40: USE AIDA WHEN COMMUNICATING

First get attention with the headline. In an e-mail, it's the subject line. In person or on the phone, you will grab their attention with the first words you utter. In a letter, it is the headline. One of the biggest challenges marketers have today is getting people's attention. Black belt marketers use powerful headlines to do so.

Once you have someone's attention, get them interested in what you have to say by showing the relevance to them. That creates desire in your prospects and gives them a reason to act. Make sure your communication follows the AIDA format for positive results. Studies show that if people read the first fifty words of your communication, they will read the rest.

MOVE
41

Feed your mind daily

MOVE 41

Feed your mind daily

M ost people accept that our physical health is based on what we eat. But when asked what determines our mental health, they usually have no idea. Black belt marketers know that mental health is determined by what goes into our minds. The great motivational speaker Zig Ziglar says it best: "You are what you are and where you are because of what has gone into your mind." Look at the five people whom you interact with the most: look at what they earn, what cars they drive, and the houses they live in. You will find you are the average of them.

Black belt marketing is not all about strategy but about mind-set—about the way you view and interpret things. Black belt marketers know the way to change their lives is to change their environment. Unless you control your environment, it will end up controlling you!

Thoughts = Actions = Results = Where you are now!

What you think about on a daily basis affects the way you act and, subsequently, the results you get.

What you think depends on what you focus on. The way to control focus is to apply filters. Don't let others' negativity get to you. Negativity is a dangerous virus that can spread easily. It is easy to catch because it is pandemic. Be careful!

Believe in your dreams, and take daily action to achieve them. The best way to control your thoughts is to avoid negative people and to consume inspirational material. Books and CDs are the best. Read about successful people. You will soon realize they were no different from you. They just believed in their dreams. I highly recommend a book called *As a Man Thinketh* by James Allen (Devross Publications). In it, Allen says: "Man is not a victim of circumstances. Circumstances are a victim of man."

We create our own circumstances in life through our thoughts and actions.

Control your destiny, your outcome, your life, your business success. Listen to CDs or MP3s in your car, which will feed the healthy and positive thoughts in your mind. Any psychologist will tell you that whatever gets into your mind will surely manifest itself. Your mind is fertile soil, so be careful what seeds you plant. And always remember

Read ------------ Believe ----------- Achieve

Those who lead always read! And the more you learn, the more you will earn.

The brain always chooses the path of least resistance. Train yourself to read or listen to twenty to thirty minutes of positive and inspirational material daily.

Black belt marketers know how to focus by asking themselves powerful questions on how to make things work out. Consequently, they find a way.

MOVE

42

Create curiosity and uncertainty

42

Create curiosity and uncertainty

B usiness is about people, and sellers must understand how people think and respond. The best salespeople are trained psychologists. Anthony Robbins actually started his career as a psychologist. One of the world's number one sales people, Dr. Donald Moine, who has reportedly sold more than five billion dollars' worth of products and services, is trained in human behavior.

These people have deep insights into human behavior, and it allows them to connect with others on a deeper level. As a black belt marketer, learn about how people think and what motivates them. Any good bookstore will have a host of information on psychology. As you earn your black belt in marketing, you will quickly learn that marketing is intimately related to the study of human behavior. After all, isn't it the behavior of people that marketers are trying to influence?

One of the key factors that gets the attention of people is curiosity. A truth of human behavior is that the human mind cannot handle uncertainty. Think about it. When do you feel uncomfortable? It happens when you are uncertain, when you don't know the exact outcome of something, or if things will work out. It's like getting into a car and discovering roadwork with no detour or diversion signs. At that moment, your mind scrambles for direction.

Knowing the power of uncertainty can help you immensely as a marketer. Once you identify a weakness, you can turn it into strength. The best marketing campaigns focus on creating uncertainty. Movie trailers create uncertainty. You want to learn more. Free seminars create uncertainty. You want to learn more. Certain phrases generate curiosity and uncertainty:

"The one simple idea most people overlook
to make money online"

"Five steps you *must* follow"

"Two things that will *absolutely* double
your sales next year"

"The biggest mistake"

"Three critical strategies"

In marketing, words convey feelings, and many of these words convey feelings of uncertainty. Humans want security. We want to know we are not missing out. In my seminars, I have people do exercises that I use for promotional material. When people read these materials—they see images of people doing funny things, such as laughing or jumping— they're confused. Why are these people doing these things? Why are they having fun? They want to know more. Uncertainty creates curiosity, and curiosity leads to action.

Why is it that if a crowd gathers somewhere, we always stop to find out what is going on? We need certainty. An ad attracts attention because it creates a level of curiosity. Humans want to be "in the know."

One of the most powerful closings is, "If you want to learn more ..." Black belt marketers use uncertainty to get the attention of others!

MOVE
43

Go direct and always get a response

MOVE 43

Go direct and always get a response

Another cost-effective way to generate sales is by using direct response advertising. This means you actually get a response from your advertising, instead of just creating awareness and interest.

The biggest complaint that I hear from business owners is: "I never make any money from advertising. I don't want to spend money on advertising." The reason for their dissatisfaction is that the advertising did not make an offer. Unless you make an offer, how can you expect people to respond?

When people read an advertisement, they want to be told what to do! People look for leadership. But most advertisements simply tell them how great a product or service is, and marketers are disappointed when they don't get a response.

Black belt marketers never run an advertisement without making an offer. It is the offer that makes people respond to the ad. Black belt marketers know the purpose of an ad is to gain permission to market, to educate, and to show value. Black belt marketers want to identify their prospects in the crowd. They want these people to raise their hands.

GET YOUR BLACK BELT IN MARKETING

Before we get down to specifics, let me share some history into direct response advertising that will help you understand its impact. Direct marketing really started with the late Claude C. Hopkins. Considered to be the father of direct marketing, he strongly believed advertising existed to sell something. He believed advertising should be measured and its results should be justified. He tracked nearly all of his ads using coupons, and tested headlines, offers, and propositions against each another.

Hopkins believed in "reason why" copy: all ads should have a reason why people respond. Why your product instead of someone else's? He used analysis to improve his ad results, driving responses and the cost effectiveness of his clients' advertising investments. This is why he was paid $185,000 per year in 1907 by Lord & Thomas owner Albert Lasker, a founding figure of modern advertising and another legend in the ad world. He knew how to use advertising to produce sales. Albert Lasker's company eventually became Draftfcb, one of the world's largest advertising agencies.

Learn from these great masters. Direct marketing is about getting a response from your ad by giving customers the reason to respond. What is the big payoff for responding to your advertisement? Your ad should be an offer. Any advertisement should get a response, even if it is only a name and contact details for your database.
Get a response by making an irresistible offer. Don't simply inform customers and prospects of what you do.

"Need air conditioning? Call 1-800-XXX-XXXX"

Ads like this appear regularly in local newspapers or in the yellow pages. Claude Hopkins taught that such ads are not acceptable. Instead, make your reader take an action.

"Free air conditioner evaluation. Call 1-800-XXX-XXXX"

Now you have made a formal offer. Your readers must make a decision. They either take advantage of it, or they don't. You have given them a reason to respond. It's proactive, not reactive. Even if they don't need you now, prospective customers may keep the advertisement for later when they do need it. Offer something of value to get a high level of response:

- Bring this ad for 15 percent off your next purchase
- Bring a friend and get 25 percent off
- Go to www … and get a free report

The goal of direct response advertising is to get a response from the money invested in generating the offer. Successful direct response advertising generates some result.

Always remember to make the most of any ads you run and you will get the maximum return on investment. You can achieve the maximum return by using direct response and soliciting a response from your advertisement, either as an immediate sale or as a lead that will eventually turn into a sale. Unless your product is under twenty-nine dollars, it is highly unlikely that people will start to send you checks based on a single advertisement.

Make creative offers. A good offer will always get a response. If you are not getting results from your advertising, you're not making a compelling offer!

If someone offered you twenty free reports or one year of free mentoring for purchasing a program, are you more likely to respond? Understand the power of direct response.

Starting today, make sure all your advertisements are direct response, which will enable you to develop a database and to develop relationships with new people.

MOVE

44

Be an optimist and opportunist

MOVE 44

Be an optimist and opportunist

If you do your marketing correctly, you will create opportunity. Successful marketers are opportunists, always looking for an opportunity to add value to the lives of others. Think of what else is possible in every activity you do. By now, your mind should be trained to see multiple opportunities in each marketing activity.

When I train sales professionals, I tell them the purpose of a sales call is not always to sell. You can call prospects to get a lot of useful sales information. For example, a person who sells scientific equipment to universities could call prospects to ask a few questions:

- Do you need more information?

- Could you refer other labs that may be interested in the equipment?

  - In the same university?

  - In another university?

- Do you have any upcoming talks scheduled?

- When are you due for a grant?

- Are there any upcoming or new labs scheduled?

- Are any other labs due for a grant?

- What are competitors doing?

- When is the best time to call again?

Ask these questions to see marketing in a broader perspective. You never know who knows who or who knows what, or where a discussion with a customer or prospect may take you. As a black belt marketer, you must develop a real interest in people. Develop a relationship. Let me give you an example. I did some consulting with a UCLA student who was impressed with the advice I had given her. She said she wanted to help me in return for my advice. I had mentioned I wanted to get on radio, to allow my message to reach a broader audience at the university. Her boyfriend ran the campus radio station, and the next thing I knew I was on UCLA radio. Was this serendipity, or the fact that as a black belt marketer, I am an opportunist? I'm trained to get the most out of each interaction with customers and prospects. To be a master marketer, you must be a master networker. To be a master networker, you must be an opportunist. Ask yourself what else is possible from an action or activity. Make a list of five additional benefits you can expect. Let's say that I give a presentation. What else could I do with it?

1. Record the talk.

2. Collect names by offering a gift to everybody who signs up.

3. Ask people who attend to refer me to people they know by offering a referral incentive.

4. Sell my products to the people who attend.

5. Offer a CD recording to the people who attend at a huge discount.

6. Ask for written testimonials from the people who attend to use on my Web site.

MOVE 44: BE AN OPTIMIST AND OPPORTUNIST

Learn to get more out of each activity, and you will be far ahead of your competition. Once you open your marketing mind, you open yourself to more marketing possibilities. There are no rules in marketing—black belt marketers create them as they go.

45

Become an expert by writing a book

MOVE 45

Become an expert by writing a book

L eaders in any field are experts by definition. And experts are well paid and respected. How can you become an expert? Show people that you have extensive knowledge on the subject matter, more than they do.

A powerful way to grow a business is to write a book. I have already written two books on marketing. If I continue to write one book a year, in eight more years, I will have written ten books. I will have shown in a relatively short time that I have a deep insight into my subject matter, and people will see me as an expert by default.

We talked about writing a book in move 9 as a way to differentiate. When you write a book, have testimonials, and appear on radio and television, you become an expert. Whatever the nature of your business, trust me, you can write a book! Writing a book is not difficult. Start by buying a recorder, and record all the ideas you have about your business, product, or service. Each idea becomes a chapter, and soon the chapters become a book!

Media attention is critical to the success of any business, and the best way to get media attention is to be seen as an expert. Writing a book is a good way to achieve expert status. When a story breaks, the media immediately looks for experts to share a perspective. Let me give you a few examples on how it works.

Tony Robbins got a call in the middle of the night from a U.S. president who needed his perspective on a situation. Why did he call Mr. Robbins? He is regarded as an expert. He has written books and given many public talks.

You could be a dry cleaner, maybe the only one who knows about the importance of allergy control. Suddenly there is a huge allergy outbreak, the biggest in U.S. history. The media needs a story, and they think the dry cleaning issue is important. You get the call! Once you are seen on television, your sales will increase! You can now write on your Web site "as seen on TV."

To become an expert, you must think and act like an expert and believe that you can become one. David Ogilvy, one of the world's most famous marketing gurus, used to say, "I am the world's best advertising man." When someone asked why, he said, "Because I say I am!" The lesson? Speak your future into existence and own it!

Whatever the size or type of your business, you have already amassed knowledge, expertise, and wisdom that people want to know about. You are an expert by the mere fact that you run a business in the field. Most companies have information lying around that could easily be converted into a book or multiple books.

Large corporations have hundreds or thousands of people working for them, and perhaps several hundred thousand articles about products and services. These articles, white papers, and reports could be made into a series of books.

It's not difficult to write a book. Write a page a day. In one year you'll have 365 pages. Books are of tremendous value to your customers. Black belt marketers will take advantage of the opportunity!

MOVE
46

Focus on serving others

MOVE 46

Focus on serving others

Many advertisements tell people about your business and may be cute. But these ads add no value to others. What do they lack?

1. What can you do for me?
2. Why should I contact you?
3. What's the value to me?

Here's an example of cute:
Alexander Locksmiths
Tel: 000-123-4567
"We have your keys to heaven. You are the key to our success."

How about
Alexander Locksmiths
"Ever been locked out? We'll be there in 20 minutes or it's free!"
24-hour service. Call 000-123-4567

Just notice the way the focus changed from the business owner to the customer. I understood why and when someone would call a locksmith, and I showed the prospect the immediate benefit and value to be gained by calling me.

The whole purpose of gaining a black belt is to disarm your competition effectively. To disarm your competition, you must learn to serve others at the highest level.

In marketing, you don't need to be cute and you don't need to be funny, you just need to be real. Show people as quickly as possible that you can add value to their lives. Be real, and your marketing will be effective. Write this down and put it in a place where you can review it daily: Be service-rendering not self-serving.

Whatever your type of business, sit down and review your message. Ask yourself three simple questions:

1. What is the key message I want to convey?

2. Are my current advertisements and promotions doing this?

3. Will my message serve others?

Marketing was designed to help serve others, and black belt marketers understand this.

MOVE

47

Go for unpaid advertising

MOVE 47

Go for unpaid advertising

There are only two forms of advertising:

1. Unpaid - Public Relations/publicity
2. Paid - Conventional advertising: print, radio, TV, etc.

Guess which is considered the most effective? Unpaid, because your customers know you don't pay for it, and it increases the value in the eyes of the customer.

I have taught you how to do effective conventional advertising, and you should. But you will get more traction with unpaid advertising. What is the difference? Advertising is what you pay for; publicity is what you pray for!

When I speak about public relations, I refer primarily to press releases. Press releases inform the media that you have a story. A press release is bait for the media. If they like it, they will call you and write an article on you. What does a press release look like? Here is one for my book *Marketing is King!*

GET YOUR BLACK BELT IN MARKETING

FOR IMMEDIATE RELEASE:
CONTACT: XXX
www.blackbeltinmarketing.com
XXX-XXX-XXXX
Learn How to Use Marketing in Everyday Life
It's Not Just for Salesmen Anymore

(SAN FRANCISCO BAY, CA) If you are on a quest for a new job or a raise, marketing guru Ali Pervez's book *Marketing is King!* (Morgan James Publishing, November 2006) is the tool you need.

Pervez is passionate about taking marketing out of the business world and into the real world. He believes marketing is broad and multi-dimensional and is able to put marketing into simple language that anyone can understand. Pervez shows how marketing is a valuable tool not just for business people but for anyone looking to make a life change. *Marketing is King!* teaches readers how to find value.

"The secret to marketing is the ability to bring value to the market-place. People buy products from you, want to build relationships with you, and hire you because it is of value to them," says Pervez.

Pervez lists the nineteen characteristics of world-class salespeople and describes how to achieve each. "You will learn that whatever you want in life is no more than a result of helping other people get what *they* want," he says.

Pervez discusses:

- How the "house of marketing" is built. The three pillars of marketing can help create perceived value in the marketplace.

- What marketing is and how it can be broken down into a set of tools that he defines as the "marketing triad." Use these tools effectively, and you can bring value to the marketplace.

- Marketing for college students. What to do once you have a degree and how to land the ideal job after graduation, with real-life case studies.

Ali Pervez is the president and chief operating officer of U Market U, a marketing services firm. He holds degrees in chemistry from the University of Manchester, U.K., and a masters degree in bio-chemistry from University College, London, as well as an MBA with distinction project in marketing from the Manchester Business School in the U.K. He has held senior marketing positions in companies ranging from start-ups to major U.S. multinationals, including Abbott Laboratories, Bio-Rad Laboratories, Sonoco Products Company, Robert Half International, and Affymetrix Inc. He has been interviewed by the BBC on the subject of marketing.

A normal advertising agency may charge several thousand dollars to write such a release, but you can easily write one yourself. Just follow the format above.

Send a press release to all the major newspapers and media folks in your area. A company called PR Newswire can assist you with this. If your release gets picked up, you will soon start appearing in newspapers at no cost—and maybe on TV too!

The value of appearing in the press is twofold:

- Instant credibility
- Opportunity to use the coverage repeatedly

Once you have been written up, obtain the reprint rights and send it out to other prospects. You now have a powerful sales piece.

I wrote the cover story for the *California Job Journal*, published April 9, 2006. I showed people how to use marketing to get a job. It did not cost me a penny. But I can use this article, accompanied by a cover letter, to send to any university career office in America. If I want to give a talk at a university, it's a powerful sales tool. I am an author who has written a published article that I did not pay for. You can do the same.

Black belt marketers know that publicity or public relations is a hundred times more powerful than conventional advertising.

MOVE

48

Document everything

MOVE 48

Document everything

Early on in my career, I had the opportunity to work with some of America's top management consultants, McKinsey & Company and Bain & Company. These folks charge a few hundred dollars an hour for their time. What I learned from these people was the ability to take good notes and to be an outstanding listener. This is the secret to their success. Contrary to popular belief, the best sales people are the best listeners, not the best talkers. They listen for opportunities to add value to other people's lives. But they don't just listen, they document. Research shows that unless you take notes, you will forget about 80 percent of what you hear over four weeks.

When large consulting companies write proposals to clients, these proposals contain what the client told them is their business problem! I know, because I have been there. People love to hear what they have said, but a small secret that black belt marketers know is that it has to be in the same syntax—exactly the same syntax—to be effective.

Let me explain. Several years ago, I was director of marketing for a start-up biotech company in the Bay Area. I was marketing the company to another large biotech company in the Bay Area. I was so good at what I did; I was able to sell the company for about $70 million within a year. How? By mastering this move: I documented everything.

During my discussion with the vice president of research of the larger biotech company, I asked, "What are you looking for? What do you think our company can offer you?"

His response: "I love your software. It has the multiplicity of constraints that we need to strengthen our platform." Then we had a general discussion. After the call, I sent him an e-mail that said something like this:

> Dear Dr. X,
>
> Thank you! I enjoyed talking to you. Having had time to think about how we can add value to your company, I would say it has to be the multiplicity of constraints we can add to your existing platform to strengthen it.
>
> Can we meet in the next two weeks to discuss this further?

It was a simple note, but it resonated well because it used the exact syntax. I was able to connect by using the same words in the same sequence that had been given to me. It was effective marketing. Within two weeks, we met again. One discussion lead to another, until the company was eventually sold.

People never forget what they say. But the trick is to repeat it exactly in the same sequence or way they said it to you. This is what we call syntax. Syntax is more important than content. Syntax makes what is said immediately relevant to the person who is listening.

The foolproof way to remember what people said and the exact way it was said (the syntax) is to document it. If you are on the phone with a prospect or customer, you can document your conversation on the computer. In a personal discussion with a customer or a prospect, take notes. Taking notes is an excellent way to show you care. It shows that you are listening and that you value what you are hearing. It shows that you are looking to add value to others.

Even small business owners should put all this information in a database after every talk with a customer. The top sales books call this the golden rule of sales:

Know thy customer!

Send birthday and anniversary cards to customers. Find things they value and build a relationship, develop a trust or bond. Put everything you know about your customer into a database.

Whatever your nature of business, say this out loud: "The more I know about them, the more they will be interested in me."

Capture and document as much information as possible in your customer database: personal details, family, things of interest, what they have bought in the past, buying preferences, and any other information you acquire that may be pertinent. Once you have enough information, you will be able to bring your customers value. You now know who they are, what they prefer, and what they value. If you don't document it, you will surely forget it.

.

MOVE
49

Do what you love

MOVE 49

Do what you love

Whenever I give a talk to college students, I tell them to write down four words that will absolutely guarantee their success in life:

Do what you love!

Marketing is about bringing value to others. It is about wanting to improve the lives of others. One of the early moves you learned in this book is to believe you have something to benefit others. This comes through doing what you love. Marketing is just your vehicle. You need confidence, because however good your product or service, it will be put to the test.

Unfortunately, we live in a world of negativity and skeptics. But if you think you can, or if you think you can't, you are correct!

In any business, acceptance usually takes time. The trust-building factor takes time. During this period, many business owners start to doubt if their product or service is really on the mark. The only thing to see you through these times is your faith and passion. Remember, when your passion is gone, your marketing is gone. Passion sells!

GET YOUR BLACK BELT IN MARKETING

True black belt marketers follow through no matter how tough times may get. If you have ever met anyone hugely successful in any business, you will find they absolutely love what they do and have total faith in their product or service and the value it can bring to others. If you are in a business just to make money, you are highly unlikely to succeed. I have been there!

If you find something you absolutely love, something you have a passion for and see as your purpose, you cannot help but succeed. People will feel your energy! I love marketing. I study it every day and am always looking for tools and resources to help others market more effectively. If you love what you do, staying at the office until 10:00 PM is no big deal. What would you do if you went home, anyway? When you do what you love, you are alive. Love the business you're in, and be passionate about it.

I have heard the sales process called a transference of feelings to make prospects and customers feel the way you feel. When they are excited, they want to get involved. So take time to ask yourself two questions: Is this what I want to do with the rest of my life? and What business do I really want to be in?

MOVE
50

Remember, everything in
marketing starts with a P

Remember, everything in marketing starts with a P

Traditional marketing books talk about the four Ps of marketing:

Product:	Have a Product to sell.
Price:	Price it correctly.
Place:	Place it in a location where people will buy it.
Promotion:	Promote it using the correct advertising medium.

But as you now know, marketing is not about the four Ps but the PV: perceived value.

Yet it seems like Ps are the basis of marketing. You will find everything in marketing starts with a P! So remember your Ps:

Two Ps of telemarketing: Always be Polite and Professional.

Two Ps of a sales mind-set: All successful salespeople know the sales profession requires Patience and Persistence.

Two Ps of managing a sale: People and Personalities.

GET YOUR BLACK BELT IN MARKETING

Two Ps of what salespeople do: Professional Persuaders.

Two Ps of sale prospecting: Sales is all about people and process. The only reason people are unsuccessful in sales is that they are either talking to the wrong People (usually suspects versus real prospects), or they are going about the sales Process incorrectly, not educating the customer of the value in purchasing a product or service.

Two Ps of sales approach: To close a sale, you need a Proposition (a value proposition) and a Premise on which the proposition is based.

Two Ps of marketing: It is often quoted that marketing is all about Packaging and Presentation.

Two Ps of marketing communication: Focus on people's Pain and Problems.

Three Ps of Customers: Refer to move 32. There are three types of customers:

Past
Present
Potential

Three Ps of asking questions: Make them Powerful, Probing, Penetrating.

Four Ps of marketing success: A good Product with a noble Purpose sold with Passion leads to Profitability.

Five Ps of marketing: Prior Preparation Prevents Poor Performance.

MOVE 50: REMEMBER, EVERYTHING IN MARKETING STARTS WITH A P

Five Ps of successful selling

Product knowledge
Persistence
Passion
People skills
Planning

These Ps should help you keep focused on how to market effectively. Always return to the Ps when you need to reset your marketing mind-set. They are a quick way to recalibrate. But black belt marketers never forget the biggest P of all:

Marketing is all about Perceived Value!

MOVE

51

Get the team behind it

MOVE 51

Get the team behind it

One the most powerful moves you can do to outperform the competition is to get a strong team behind a product launch or a major marketing campaign. It's the old three musketeers saying: "All for one and one for all."

Everyone in the company has one goal, to bring perceived value to the marketplace. The best organizations simply have the best teams not the best people. Teams put the organizational goals above their own; teams will do anything to make the project successful; teams respect each member's unique knowledge and experience.

Having done several product launches that have gone on to make several millions of dollars in sales, I can tell you the atmosphere in the best team meetings is what I imagine Mission Control Houston was like when NASA first landed a man on the moon. The whole team was behind the project. The team that pulls together will always pull it off.

Irrespective of the size of your organization, at the end of the day the best team wins. Even in a small company of three people, everyone should be involved in decisions, input, and feedback. Unless each person is 120 percent committed to a marketing program, it will not succeed. Your business is only as strong as its weakest link.

A good team is formed when people have respect for each other's knowledge and skill sets. Marketing people are no better than anyone else; they simply do the front-end work that requires them to interface with the market and customers.

Even as a sole proprietor, your team is made up of external advisors: an accountant, close friends, mentors, and so forth. None of us lives on an island, and we must surround ourselves with quality people committed to our success.

In marketing more brains equals more power! Napoleon Hill, the famous motivational speaker, calls this the Mastermind Principle. Successful people surround themselves with powerful minds, people who can share ideas to stimulate thought. Whatever the size of the company, assemble a core team from different areas to assess what is needed to ensure success of your mission. Some of the best multinational corporations I have worked for have a core group of people who understand three ideas:

- All members' opinions are equally valued.
- Failure is not an option.
- All the knowledge needed is in the team.

I have launched seven successful products during my marketing career, and each has gone on to make several million dollars in sales. I had the right teams, people I trusted and respected. Everyone focused on doing whatever was necessary to ensure the product's success.

The team pulls together for one goal: to ensure the product being launched or the marketing campaign is a huge success. Black belt marketers understand the importance of teamwork.

MOVE

52

Capture those million
dollar ideas

MOVE 52

Capture those million dollar ideas

As a businessperson and entrepreneur, you continuously have ideas. The best ideas usually come in the shower, right? The ideas are so clear that you know if you implemented them, you'd make a million dollars! We all get these ideas from time to time.

In fact, the only difference between your idea and someone else's million dollar idea is that they wrote it down and took action on it! I believe our Creator is kind. He treats us all equally and gives us all equal opportunities. But I also believe that if you don't take advantage of your ideas, you will stop getting them.

Whatever the nature of your business, you will have ideas on how to improve it. Maybe you saw something or talked to someone, maybe the idea came to you in the shower, in the car, or in the middle of the night. You are certain that the idea could change the course of your life. But if you don't write it down within a few hours, it will be gone forever.

That's why you should always carry a voice recorder and notepad with you. When you get the idea, record it, write it down, and make it a weekly habit to review both your oral and written notes.

GET YOUR BLACK BELT IN MARKETING

I got a lot of ideas for my books in the shower. As soon as I leave the shower, I write them down. A mentors once told me: "If you don't immediately write those ideas or jail them, you are not going to get anymore!"

There has been much written about subliminal thought and the power of the subconscious mind. I have read much on it, and what I can share with you as your marketing master is that your mind has the answer to any problem you may have. You just need to challenge it. Don't worry about how you will achieve your goal; you need to just focus on why you need to achieve it. Psychologists tell us the how will appear (this is the answer from the subconscious). Your job is to focus on the why. When you get the answer, write it down.

All businesses start with a simple idea that one day becomes reality. A book starts as a train of thought, ideas that are captured and then strung together in a logical format. When people ask me how I came up with eighty-one moves, I tell them I committed myself to find eighty-one of the most revenue-generating moves. As they came along, I wrote them down. And they just kept coming. Black belt marketers recognize that the answers will appear once the commitment is made!

MOVE
53

Marketing is a set of tools

MOVE 53

Marketing is a set of tools

Y ou know marketing is about bringing perceived value to the marketplace. All of the strategies I have shared with you lead to this powerful move. A black belt marketer understands that marketing is no more than a set of tools.

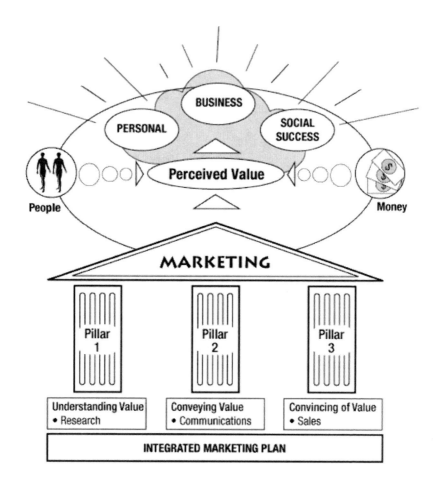

Each of these tools has a defined purpose in marketing:

Market research
Marketing communications
Sales

1. MARKET RESEARCH: WHERE IS THE OPPORTUNITY TO ADD VALUE?

Market research is a tool that determines where the opportunities are to add value. Market research shows you what your market truly values and is prepared to pay for if you can deliver it. Market research is the heart of all quality marketing campaigns. If you know what your customers value and are prepared to pay for, then you have presold them. It becomes a matter of just delivering the goods. Selling becomes easy and ideally unnecessary.

There are two forms of market research: primary and secondary. Primary is when you interview people directly; secondary comes as information from published sources.

2. MARKETING COMMUNICATIONS: SHOW ME THE VALUE!

Marketing communication comes into play only when you know what people want and value. Only when you understand what they value can you communicate a quality message. This can be a letter, a television ad, a print ad, or any other medium that communicates the message. This is where creativity comes in. Creative people are designers and copywriters who assist with the delivery of the message to the intended audience. People should respond immediately to your campaign once you clearly understand what the market wants, right? Unfortunately, this does not always happen. Why?

Most advertising or marketing campaigns are done without doing market research.

Black belt marketers understand that there are no shortcuts. Spend the time and money doing research before telling the world about your product or service! If you know what people truly want, your advertisement should generate a response.

3. Sales: Convince me that you have what I want and value

The final tool at your disposal is sales. Sales is the art of persuasion. Persuade people what you have is of value to them and can improve their lives. Help people make an informed and intelligent decision. If you have done your market research correctly, you should know exactly what the market wants. Develop sales literature with the correct messaging as a supporting tool. Then show people it is to their benefit to purchase the product or service.

When you use these tools in an integrated way, you will truly be a black belt marketer. In my book *Marketing is King!* I show how these tools come together to form what I call the "house of marketing." These are the basic elements of any quality marketing plan.

MOVE
54

Reach for the stars

54

Reach for the stars

The great advertising genius Leo Burnett, who created icons such as the Pillsbury Doughboy and Tony the Tiger, is quoted as saying: "When you reach for the stars you may not quite get one, but you won't come up with a handful of mud either."

Never lower your standards. I certainly never thought I could write a book or get it endorsed, but I was able to do it. Nothing could stop me except my belief in myself. Once I started to believe, I started to achieve. Black belt marketers aim high.

It takes the same amount of effort to achieve a big goal as it does to achieve a small one. So go for a big one! Your business is only limited by your vision. This book exposes you to time-tested and proven revenue-generating strategies. They will work if you are prepared to work them.

It can get boring when business is not growing. When you start to apply the moves in this book, you will have no time to be bored. Business and life regain their vibrancy when your goal is to help people.

GET YOUR BLACK BELT IN MARKETING

This is a short and simple move, but an important one: always grow. Ray Kroc, the founder of McDonald's said, "When you learn, you grow, and when you stop growing, you're dead."

MOVE

55

Know what management is

MOVE 55

Know what management is

As a black belt marketer, you are in management. You manage the marketing function of your business. But what do you really do? What is management? The late Peter Drucker, the legendary management guru, defined management as predictability. Notice another P of marketing (move 50). Management is your ability to predict with a high level of confidence the outcome of an activity.

As an executive, owner, or top executive, you make decisions. These decisions are based on the confidence that you will gain a positive outcome. You predict the outcome.

Management = Predictability = Quality decisions = Money

Testing is the quick and dirty of marketing. Through testing you find out what works and what doesn't. Large corporations have a board of directors and you may have a mentor, so you can predict with a high degree of confidence the result of a certain investment. This is based on the experience that they have in similar business situations.

GET YOUR BLACK BELT IN MARKETING

Management and marketing are all about predictability. Few of your competitors know what management is, although this is what they do for a living. Master this move, and you will pass them by.

Top management at large corporations spends days, weeks, and maybe months reviewing data before making a decision. They try to predict the outcome of a decision. The market data is there to help them.

In the same way, once you know what to do as a marketing manager or executive, your job becomes easier. While most of the competition does not know what managers do, as a black belt marketer, your goal is to make quality marketing decisions to drive revenue through the door.

Know that small things make a big difference

MOVE 56

Know that small things make a big difference

Many business owners wish they could make one singular change that would alter the course of business. It is highly unlikely this will happen. But small things do make a big difference in business.

A lot of the moves in this book are small changes that when implemented over time can certainly have a profound impact on any business. Change is a gradual process, but incremental change happens over a long period. Let me ask you a question: Could you make a one-degree shift in the way you market every day? If so, how long would it take to have your marketing headed in the opposite direction?

1 degree a day
180 degrees in 180 days
180 days to head in the opposite direction

Great changes are always achieved in incremental steps. The secret to change is incremental steps. Any successful person has worked hard over a long period. Change is not an overnight process. We do not become wealthy by watching TV. In fact, TV is an income suppressant. To become successful, use your time effectively and take daily small steps toward your goals. There are no shortcuts in marketing.

Remember to be disciplined in doing the small things. Pay attention to each move mentioned in this book, and master them. Let your competitors continue to think that one change will alter the course of their marketing. Yet powerful marketing comes when all the small elements of your marketing strategy start to work together.

- A simple headline change can increase a response to an advertisement twenty-one times over.

- Ask existing customers, "Who else do you know?" Formal referral systems can double your sales.

- Offer customer appreciation gifts or cards to create loyalty to make customers buy more and buy more often.

- Offer value items so people buy more.

Black belt marketers recognize that small changes add up over time and can completely alter the course of their businesses.

MOVE
57

Make doing business with you
fun and exciting!

MOVE 57

Make doing business with you fun and exciting!

People buy products or services because they improve their lives. Some are a necessity, others a luxury. Prospects always have a choice: Why should they choose you? As a master marketer, you know it is because you offer more value than the competition. You care for your customers more than the competition.

Value is broken down into two parts:

Value = Tangible + Intangible

Tangible	Relates to the economic benefits of purchasing your product or service.
Intangible	Deals with emotions gained by purchasing what you have to offer.

The reason people choose your product or service over someone else's is they see more value, both tangible and intangible, in your product or service than in anyone else's. Most business owners think that tangible value is most important: the product itself, what it does, the money it can save. But black belt marketers know this truth: intangible value (the soft side) is of equivalent, if not more, value to customers.

Intangible value refers to relationships, gifts, and the fun people have in doing business with you. Keep customers informed, educated, and entertained. We all need to make a living, and a businessperson does this by selling products and services. But what if we can have fun at the same time? What if you could make your customers feel important? What if you could build solid, long-lasting relationships with your customers and make it fun for them to do business with you? But how can you make doing business with you a fun event?

Keep surprising your customers. Send them cards every month of the year! Black belt marketers take advantage of every opportunity to build long-term and lasting relationships with customers. Take advantage of the following events:

January	New Year's
February	Valentine's Day, President's Day
March	St. Patrick's Day
April	April Fools' Day, Easter
May	Mother's Day
June	Father's Day, Graduations, Weddings
July	Independence Day
August	Back to School
September	Labor Day, Grandparents' Day
October	Halloween
November	Thanksgiving
December	Christmas, Hanukkah

The cost of a card? Maybe a dollar or two, but the impact? Priceless and long-lasting. If you don't think of your customers, they will surely not think of you. Regular mailings are not only effective but memorable, because you can include a personal note. As long as you are genuine in your approach, people will love you. Black belt marketers are genuine and see all customers as part of their extended family (move 3).

These types of mailings can also be done through e-mail. The purpose of the mailings is to show intangible value—value that cannot be quantified but has a high degree of importance to customers. Black belt marketers are masters of psychology and know everyone wants to feel important.

Whatever your type of business, your customers will greatly value that you have taken time to think about them on a personal level at least once per month. These special mailings should be a part of your marketing budget. Most of your competitors will hardly think of these things. When was the last time you got a Thanksgiving or Christmas card from someone you did business with? And when you did, how did it make you feel about them?

Marketing is a continuous process of adding value to your customers and prospects, with the goal of converting them to clients. Set up a consistent program to do mailings. Business is about loyalty, and loyalty comes through building close relationships with your customers. These mailings allow you to build trust quickly with customers.

A local pizza store sends a pizza to a school math class once a month. It costs a few dollars, but the impact is long-lasting. The kids send thank-you letters to the pizza store, saying they will always buy that particular brand. It's a great example of making it fun to do business with you.

Black belt marketers know marketing is about making the right investments. One of the best investments you can make is making doing business with you fun and exciting!

MOVE
58

Make friends with strangers

58

Make friends with strangers

I showed you in move number twenty-three how to make your advertising work for you and how effective advertising is a black belt move that will generate sales revenue for your organization.

In this move, we are going to talk about the alternatives that you have when you choose to advertise, as well as discuss how advertising is not always about getting the sale. Although we have been conditioned to think that advertising is all about getting sales, the most powerful form of advertising is when it is used not to sell, but to generate sales leads or to get a direct response.

But this is the opposite of what most people do when they advertise. We learned earlier that as a black belt marketer, you are going to do a lot of things that are often the opposite of what conventional and traditional marketers do.

This move is one of the more advanced in this book because it challenges your understanding of human psychology, which, as you now know, is the basis of marketing.

What is the purpose of advertising? The majority of people might think that advertising is used to create awareness and generate sales. Large corporations and people with an MBA would say that it is to create branding because they are taught to think more strategically.

Only a black belt marketer can tell you that advertising has one of three goals:

- Make an immediate sale

- Create awareness and branding that will lead to a sale

- Generate a lead that will eventually convert into a sale.

In all three scenarios, the purpose, or end game, of advertising is to get a sale. But the steps and time frame are different. Now take a guess at which you think is the most powerful of all three strategies above? Yes, to use advertising to generate a lead. A lead, once qualified, can be put into a database (move nineteen)that can then be worked (move twenty) and continually sold to so that you don't just sell once, but sell frequently, and this lead can then refer you to others (move ten). Now you are seeing how the moves come together.

If you run an advertisement to generate a sale, in most instances it is usually a promotion. Here we are looking at the "how to sell snow to an Eskimo" example. If you write a quality ad (like we did in move number twenty-three) and make a compelling enough offer, you can sell snow to the Eskimo. But the question becomes, would the Eskimo ever buy from you again? *If you make a sale, and your customer only buys once, you have in essence a promotion, not a business.*

Most business owners think that running one advertisement will make them very wealthy. And this is the mindset of instant gratification. This is taking a very short-term view of marketing.

But what all black belt marketers understand is that unless your offering is less than $29.99, it is highly unlikely that you will be able to sell it using a single advertisement. People are prepared to risk up to $29.99, if you have a reasonably good guarantee to go with it.

Beyond this, they need education, involvement, and your personal interaction in order to build a sense of trust and make them feel that they are making the right decision (move number four). The biggest reason that people don't buy is because they fear making a mistake.

Marketers that think that they can simply run an ad and make a profit are *traders in for the quick buck.*

The other alternative—one that is used by large corporations—is creating a brand and trying to take ownership of your mindshare. Here businesses want you to think of them when you are ready to make your purchase decision. Large multinational corporations will spend millions of dollars on advertising because they want to own a portion of the consumers' minds. They understand the psychology of marketing. When you are at a store and you are ready to make that final decision, you ask yourself, "Which brand should I buy?" You mind will often flash a picture of the last ad that you saw, and your decision is made.

Institutional advertising, contrary to all belief, does actually work. It works because the trust is built by seeing the same brand several times over the course of the course of several months or years. And you begin to make an emotional connection with it. It makes you say, "If they are advertising so much, it must be good." And once you buy it, institutional marketers are able to make you keep buying it, by keeping it in your minds eye, through repeated advertising.

But this strategy takes deep pockets and is over the long haul. Quality brands are built over a decade of continuous institutional advertising.

Finally there is the strategy that is used by black belt marketers , and that is using advertising to simply generate leads or direct response advertising (move number forty three). *You run the ad to learn more about your audience, not to tell them how great you are.* You are asking them to share information about themselves. The purpose is to get people out there to raise their hand and say, " I think I need your help." You want people to call to get more information so you can capture their contact information and qualify them. And, of course, build a relationship with them.

All yellow pages ads are about lead generation; they are not intended for direct sale. The Internet or any classified ads are also for lead generation. And only if you are a black belt marketer will you have made this connection.

But how do you go from a contact to a sale? By developing a relationship. By using the CRTS strategy

Contact ---- Relationship ----- Trust ----- Sale   (CRTS)

As a black belt marketer, you now know that all money in marketing is made on the back end, not the front end. A contact, such as a business card, has no front end value, but once qualified and educated, it can become an immense value. This comes through making a relationship. Only when you are able to develop a relationship and trust can you make a sale.

A contact via an advertisement, a business card collected at a networking event, an e-mail address collected on your web site—these are all simply leads! You now need to work these leads into a sale over the next several months! The only difference with a Web lead is that it is usually well qualified, as they found you based on a keyword search, so they are in essence a well-qualified prospect.

The important point to remember is that there is still a long way to go from getting someone's business card, a lead over an internet, or a response to an ad to getting money out of his or her wallet! All black belt marketers know that there are no shortcuts. And it takes a lot of patience to follow through with leads (notice another P of marketing, from move number fifty). You need to run through the trust-building cycle (move twenty four).

MOVE 58: MAKE FRIENDS WITH STRANGERS

The irony is that most traditional marketers know that they really should be focused on using advertising to develop leads, but they do not take advantage of this. Why? Because our study of human psychology shows us that *the mind always follows the path of least resistance.*

Advertisers find it hard to tell their clients that they have to spend several thousands of dollars to run an ad that will, at best, only produce leads that now require a "fresh new marketing campaign," such as a series of follow-up letters, e-mails, and direct contacts. They would prefer to run an ad and hope that people will buy products immediately or perhaps purchase later through their branding efforts. *Again, the mind always follows the path of least resistance.*

But as a black belt marketer, you know how to control your mind and do what is right in the long term, which is to use advertising to generate a lead and then work that lead over a few months, as well was qualify and develop relationships with the ones that are the most promising. Convert prospects to customers, customers to clients, and clients to advocates that continue to buy and refer you.

When all is said and done, business is about developing and managing relationships, and these relationships are, for the most part, with strangers. But as we grew up, what did our parents teach us? "Don't make friends with strangers." Unless you are a black belt marketer, you will continue to fear making friends with strangers, and you will look down on networking, when in reality, making friends with strangers and networking are the number one revenue-developing strategies in this book. As a black belt marketer, you think very differently than anyone else. In black belt marketing, your Networth = Network!

The Internet is the best example of making friends with strangers: people are buying and selling from people they have never met. If you want to make millions on the Internet, you must become a master of making friends with strangers very quickly.

MOVE

59

Strengthen your marketing vocabulary

59

Strengthen your marketing vocabulary

N ow you know marketing is about communication of value to others and the ability to show others the value they can gain by doing business with you. Let's talk about your marketing vocabulary: the primary tools for marketing professionals are the words they choose to use. A powerful headline will stop you in stride, and a powerful headline is no more than a selection of carefully chosen words. Words create emotions that result in people taking action. So it logically follows the choice of words is one of the biggest secrets held by marketing gurus.

To strengthen your marketing vocabulary, these key words should become part of your daily communication. These words will make you stand out from the crowd. They are proven to stimulate emotion and empower people to take action. Use them, and immediately see a change in the way people respond.

Absolutely	Astounding
Amazing	Bargain
Beautiful	Crammed
Enormous	Fantastic
Fascinating	Free

Full	Genuine
Gigantic	Good
Happy	Helpful
How	Huge
Immediately	Improved
Incredible	Lavishly
Lifetime	Love
New	Now
Popular	Powerful
Practical	Proven
Rare	Remarkable
Secrets	Special
Strong	Successful
Truly	Unconditional
Unique	You
Yours	

Notice these words are mainly adjectives. Use only a few of these carefully chosen words in your e-mails, letters, and advertisements to have an immediate effect on your audience. Words create emotions, and emotions are what make people buy.

Phrases such as "Good Selling!" and "Happy Selling!" get your attention, connect with you, and engage you! Like all the best moves, this move simple and will have an immediate and profound effect on your marketing.

MOVE

60

Know the one percent rule
of direct marketing.
Volume = Lift!

MOVE 60

Know the one percent rule of direct marketing. Volume = Lift!

Most businesses make a huge mistake when it comes to marketing. They don't understand the amount of effort it takes to get others' attention. Consequently, they underbudget their marketing requirements, which renders the marketing ineffective. Black belt marketers understand that in direct mail, 1.5 to 2 percent of the audience will respond. However good your offer, not everyone will take advantage of it. You need massive volume to capture a small number of well-qualified prospects.

Let me give you an example. A recent conference I attended in the San Francisco Bay Area marketed to about ten million people through

- Billboards
- Radio
- Television
- Letters
- Print advertising
- E-mails

GET YOUR BLACK BELT IN MARKETING

This event was truly life changing, with great information and speakers. It was affordable, too. With aggressive promotion, guess how many people attended the conference? Approximately ten thousand. In this case, only 0.1 percent of the people marketed to came to the event. The lesson is that no matter how good your offer is, you need volume to get lift.

Whenever you spend money on a direct marketing campaign, expect a one percent response rate. Or don't bother! It's tough to get people's attention these days.

One percent of the audience will respond, while the other 99 percent will have other ideas:

- Not trust you—Don't believe you can bring them the value they want.

- Not even read your offer—They are just too busy!

It's nothing personal. The way that nearly all businesses grow is through referrals and word of mouth (move 10).

A marketing promotion campaign is just like gambling. The odds are not in your favor. Most people do not budget enough money to do an effective campaign. Sending a few hundred letters will not make it happen for you. Giving out a few hundred samples will not make it happen for you. You need massive volume to make any marketing campaign successful. Let's look at more examples to prove the point.

Major pharmaceutical companies give out thousands of samples to doctors' offices every month!

You cannot get a lift in marketing until you have volume. Volume = Lift

MOVE 60: KNOW THE 1% RULE OF DIRECT MARKETING

Study the table below to determine your lift factor.

Customers required	Volume required for 1% response rate
10	1,000
100	10,000
1,000	100,000
10,000	1,000,000

It is expensive to get customers. Some statistics claim it takes seven repeated interactions, others say five. Either way, people will not take you seriously unless you gain mind share—you are able to make them think of you, and you only, when they need a solution to their problem. This comes through volume with a value message.

Change your mind-set. Yes, it takes a significant volume to get lift in marketing. Eight out of ten new companies fail because they underestimate the marketing costs to get their first customers.

PostcardMania, a small postcard company in Florida, has grown 289 percent over the last three years, just by understanding the one percent rule. They send out about seventy-two thousand postcards a week (yes, per week) to get prospects. They have been in business for about ten years and do about twenty million dollars in sales because they understand the relationship between volume and lift. When they started, they mailed only one thousand postcards per week. But then these owners found a direct correlation between volume and response.

The secret to the one percent rule is to get both volume and repetition working for you. Nearly all companies that struggle with marketing grossly underestimate the volume required to show people the value they have to offer. You need to send high-quality information regularly over a long time before people will get the message.

GET YOUR BLACK BELT IN MARKETING

An old marketing saying goes like this: "For an effective marketing campaign, all you need is a good list and a great offer." Many of your competitors will send maybe fifty or a hundred mailing pieces once and hope the phone will ring. It will not happen. You can never over-communicate in marketing.

L. Ron Hubbard, the founder of Scientology, says, "You get paid in line with the attention you get." To get people's attention these days requires massive effort. It's nothing personal, just business as usual. As you master this move, remember you need both momentum and a good message to be successful in marketing. Don't be shy, or you will lose out. Volume and repetition is the only way to get attention (and to get business)!

Use questions to define the
buying criteria

61

Use questions to define the buying criteria

You now know the result of quality marketing is a sale, because this marketing creates significant value for your prospects. Once you understand what they want and value, it is simply a matter of relaying your solution. How do you gain an understanding of what customers want and value? Through your ability to ask quality questions.

The world's top marketers know that questions are the answer. The ability to ask quality questions tells you what people want to buy and allows you to identify prospects quickly.

Questions are your answers to successful marketing. "All world-class sales people ask Powerful, Probing, and Penetrating questions." (Again notice the Ps in move 50.)

Most sales books tell you to ask open-ended questions, which require more than a yes or no answer. Black belt marketers know to ask powerful, probing, and penetrating questions to get to the root cause of the problem, just like doctors. Remember, products and services exist to solve people's problems. As a black belt marketer, you are not just a listener, you are digging for more information.

The person asking the questions is always in control of the conversation. Questions control the focus of what people think about. Here are a few examples.

RETAIL STORE

When someone walks into a retail store, the clerk usually asks, "Can I help you?"

But the black belt marketer might say, "You're in the video recorder area of our store. Can you tell me what you are looking for in a video recorder? I can then help you identify the best one for you."

Notice how the last comment focuses on defining the buying criteria. When you know this, you can map a solution.

VITAMIN MANUFACTURING COMPANY

Now let's look at a manufacturing company. Usually sales representatives simply do data dumps, which is providing all the facts and figures that they know about their product or service to prospects. Or they point out the features of a product or service and expect people to buy. They usually say, "Here's what this does. Would you like to buy it?"

The black belt marketer might say, "I notice you currently use vitamin supplements. What do you particularly like about the supplements you use? What benefit do you expect to gain from them?"

Once you know the purchasing criteria, you can make an informed recommendation by saying: "Based on what you told me, you might want to consider our product for the following reasons. You mentioned your primary objective is to gain antioxidants. Our supplement has …"

Notice how you sell by educating people, and helping them make informed and intelligent decisions. Whatever the nature of your business, you must solve particular problems. And until you can clearly articulate the problem (define the buying criteria), there is no way to solve it.

344

MOVE 61: USE QUESTIONS TO DEFINE THE BUYING CRITERIA

All prospects and customers give you the opportunity to make money every time you meet them if you ask these prospects the right questions and listen carefully to their responses. You then have the opportunity to make a sale.

MOVE
62

Maximize your
purchasing power

62

Maximize your purchasing power

I n today's competitive business arena, the only way to succeed is by getting more out of each action and activity you do. We have talked a lot about value and about how to bring value to the market. That market is always looking for maximum value. Now, I am going to show you how to use value to increase your purchasing power.

Marketing, as you know, is all about perceived value.

Cost  Perceived value

People buy based on the perceived value they expect to get in purchasing a product or service. Once you know this, it should change the way you buy, so you can buy more for your dollar. Let's study the example below:

Let's say my CD costs	$5	
Let's say it sells for	$20	Perceived value created through marketing
Profit	$15	

GET YOUR BLACK BELT IN MARKETING

What if I go to a restaurant to do marketing? I tell the owner about how to market and give her some ideas about how to use marketing to double sales in sixty days, at little or no incremental cost. I say just one strategy from my CD (like referrals) can do it. I show the benefits, the results, and the outcome she can gain from the CD.

I do this while I am waiting for my food, and, when the bill comes, it totals $100. I ask the owner if he's interested in the CD. "I have all the ideas on this CD. You can listen to it again and again."

He says, How much is it?"

I say, I normally sell it for $20. I have a few in my car, and you may want to give some to your friends in business as well."

We agree. I give him five CDs and get a $100 meal.

In reality, I got a $100 meal for $25. I maximized my purchasing power five times over!

This is conventional bartering (or trade), and it works. It's a time-honored tradition. I have conducted bartering many times to maximize my purchasing power, because I understand marketing and perceived value.

All black belt marketers prefer a trade to a buy. I also bartered with a television station. I gave them marketing consulting services based on my rate of a few hundred dollars an hour. They gave me airtime. My time is worth whatever I think it is. It costs a tenth of what I charge. But because I have written two books, I have a lot of perceived value in the market. You can do the same thing!

Irrespective of your type of business, you sell based on perceived value. If you know this, you can immediately maximize your purchasing power by bartering.

MOVE 62: MAXIMIZE YOUR PURCHASING POWER

Just think of all the people who can benefit from your product or service, and then offer it in return for a product or service you want from them. Get paid on what others think it is worth to them.

Some examples below may help:

Company type	Product/service offered	Possible trade
Dry cleaner	Clean clothes	Accounting services
DIY/repair person	Home repairs	Vacations using travel agent
Health-care company	Vitamins	A car, using car dealer
Car dealer	Cars	Radio airtime

The combinations are limited only by your mind. Bartering boils down to what you have versus what you want. Black belt marketers know how to make the trade.

Customer Service =
Marketing + Product
Development

MOVE 63

Customer Service = Marketing + Product Development

Good customer service today is considered to give a lot of lip service. Of course, we all know we should be kind and polite so customers will not spread negative words of mouth, and we know how powerful words can be (move ten). As a black belt marketer, however, you understand the true potential of a customer service function.

You see customer service as both product development and marketing. Use feedback from customers to continually improve the performance of your product (product development) and to get referrals (marketing) from satisfied customers. As we learned in move 6, feedback can only make you better. The best feedback is from the market: how you can improve your offering so they will tell others about it.

In many ways, customer service is marketing, because marketing is simply the opportunity to add value. Any occasion to talk with a customer offers the opportunity to add value. One of the most powerful things black belt marketers can do is use customer feedback to develop new collateral and sales letters. How does this work?

When a customer service representative talks to a customer, that customer says what he likes and dislikes about the product or service.

355

When this information is documented (we talked about the importance of documentation in move 48) and when you communicate with the customer again, you can show you truly understand the problem. In this way, you connect and build rapport.

Everyday marketers assume sales people are the most important in the company. To a high degree, this is true. But black belt marketers know that anyone with customer interface time has the ability to bring value. Customer service folks spend at least as much time with customers as sales professionals, but how many companies take advantage of this fact?

Black belt marketers see the world differently than other people. You have X-ray vision; you leverage every action and seize every opportunity. You know the power of customer service: It can, to mention a few benefits:

1.   Build your pyramid of referrals (move 10).

2.   Give you feedback for the next million dollar product.

3.   Provide copy points to make your marketing more effective.

Leveraging your customer service department can have a profound impact on business. Documenting feedback from existing customers will provide information to approach new prospects. You now understand what sells and the likely objections and can handle them upfront.

Remember, conventional customer service is important. These facts come from the National Association for Retail Marketing Services (NARMS):

- Ten customers are lost for every one complaint of poor service.

- It costs seven times more to get a new client than to keep an existing one.

- Thirteen percent will tell more than twenty people about their bad experience.

MOVE 62: CUSTOMER SERVICE=MARKETING+PRODUCT DEVELOPMENT

- Ninety percent of unhappy clients will not do business with a company again.

- Ninety-five percent of customers *will* return if an issue is resolved quickly and efficiently.

These facts and figures apply directly to retail establishments, but you will find they apply to all types of businesses, plus or minus ten percent.

Business is not just about selling; it is about the after-sale, a continuous and on-going process. Anyone can get a customer, but you want a happy customer, one who will want to continue to buy from you, become a client, and refer you to others. The experience your customer has with a product or service is what ultimately makes it (and you) successful. Marketing is a catalyst to get things going quickly. It's the continuum to customer service, and ensures the opportunities to add value continually. Happy customers buy more and refer more. Feedback allows you to improve on your customer service.

Five keys to make your customer service exceptional include

1. Want to serve others. Good customer service begins with a positive view of customers. This is a state of mind, wanting your customers to enjoy the experience of doing business with you and wanting to help them make the right decisions.

2. Constant and never-ending feedback from customers. Know what your customers want and value, and change and evolve your product or service accordingly.

3. Respond to customer problems. When customers' problems become your problem, you make money. Take a real interest in their problems.

4. Develop on-going and repeat relationships. Long-term relationships are the only way to develop a long-term business. The more

you know about your customers, the more interested they will be in you. Know about both their business and personal lives.

5. Always exceed customer expectations. The greatest opportunity to satisfy and retain customers is to exceed expectations. Under-promise and over-deliver. Do more than a customer expects, and you will build trust quickly.

As a black belt marketer, you must practice these moves regularly.

MOVE
64

Tell stories

MOVE

64

Tell stories

D on't forget who you market to! Your customers are ordinary people just like you and me. Black belt marketers treat people like people— like best friends. They understand people have feelings and are able to relate to them. Some of the most effective communicators are storytellers, who are able to relate with their audience. Do you remember how much you enjoyed listening to stories as a young child?

Our minds work in pictures. When someone relates a story, we create mind pictures. As the story gets deeper, the pictures became more vivid. All our thoughts are translated into pictures, so, when someone tells a story, they are making a movie in our minds. Psychologists and top-notch marketing professionals know and use stories to effectively market, and now you can too. They also know that

Facts tell, but stories sell!

Next time you have a conversation with a prospect or customer, explain it in the form of a story. Let me give you an example of this incredibly powerful move in action. Let's say I am trying to sell you a course on real estate investing. "Mr. Customer, I would like to show you how one of my students benefited from using this home study course. He was only twenty years old and had never had any experience in real estate investing. In using this home study course, he was able to buy his dream house within thirty days of purchasing the course. Can you imagine how he felt?"

As you read this, certain things happened in your mind:

1. You picture a twenty-year-old.

2. You imagine him wandering around, trying to figure things out.

3. You imagine him sitting at a desk, reading.

4. You see a beautiful, million-dollar home.

5. You see him dancing around and celebrating!

This is a psychological move based on the way the mind works. Marketing creates feelings through vivid images created through careful word selection.

Remember, storytelling is selling. We all love a good story. People are often interested in how I got my book published with a New York publisher and all the trials and tribulations I went through in the process. When I give a presentation, I end up telling the whole story. Next time you have a conversation with someone, tell that person a story. Make it vivid, colorful, and entertaining.

Storytelling will allow you to build relationships quickly (move 4).

Stories can be integrated into any of your marketing campaigns, such as newspaper ads or formal or casual presentations. Stories work well because they can easily be integrated with the primary objective of marketing: to educate your customers and prospects on the value you offer.

Here are some good story start lines:

"Let me tell you about ..."
"I once had a customer who ..."
"I would like to share a story with you ..."
"Let me give you a real-life example of how this works ..."
"You are not going to believe this!"

Stories make learning fun. And black belt marketers know that when it's fun, people remember. So turn your offer into an Oscar-winning movie or story. People sometimes lead boring lives, and they go to the movies to escape. Turn your product or service into a movie ticket, and you could have a box office hit!

MOVE
65

Hire the best

65

Hire the best

One of the biggest assets of any organization is its people. A company is no more than a collection of people, and, although they don't show up in the financial report, they are the core. The best companies are the best companies because they have the best people. The products or services we buy are the result of the people who developed, designed, and marketed them. When a business owner or executive hires, she hires the future of the company.

A company may be formed with a name, but certain key people who are committed to make it successful will often turn that name into a brand. McKinsey & Company, one of the world's most influential management consulting companies, was formed by James McKinsey in 1926. In 1933, he hired Marvin Bower, who held both a JD and an MBA from Harvard University. McKinsey adamantly believed that management consulting should be held to the same high standards for professional conduct as law and medicine. Nearly all of the people hired to build McKinsey came from the top 1 percent of students at the top business schools around the country. The company follows this practice to this day and remains a world leader in the field.

GET YOUR BLACK BELT IN MARKETING

The worst mistake any business owner can make is to hire the wrong person. Black belt marketers know that smart people don't cost money; they actually save it. Remember the golden rule for hiring: hire slowly, and remove quickly if they don't perform.

Take your time to hire and ensure you hire the best. Hiring, like marketing, is about making an investment. The best investment a company can make is to hire the right person for the job. That new hire will not only do the job but a whole lot more.

I once interviewed a billionaire who started a company from scratch in the San Francisco Bay Area. I asked him, "What is your secret to success?" His answer: "I hired the right people."

You have no challenges in life, as long as you know your limitations. Hire people who have the skills you do not have. In marketing, great copywriters and designers are worth their weight in gold. They can design and write materials that sell for you!

Local universities and colleges are a great source for employees. It is not by chance that some of the world's most famous companies have some of the best people on the staff. The management was highly selective in choosing future management.

Take your time when it comes to hiring. Be selective. The best people are those who truly want to make a difference. Use a standard ninety-day probation period. However good someone looks on paper or checks out with references, you just never know. Next, establish clear goals. Set thirty-, sixty-, and ninety-day goals from day one. Employees need clear direction. Without expectations, they will simply do their own thing.

Hiring smart people is key, but managing effectively opens their true potential. Once goals are set, let employees do their thing. Provide whatever support, counsel, and infrastructure is needed. Never micromanage! Review after ninety days. If they are not performing, sit them down for a coaching session.

Black belt marketers know how to find talented people with the skills to make a difference in business. Intellectual capital is brainpower to take your organization to the next level.

Once you have the best people on your team, keep them motivated. Thank them and validate them. Surprise them with gifts. You will be amazed how a small, occasional gift will help to open up true potential.

MOVE
66

Anything you can do,
I can do better

66

Anything you can do,
I can do better

Is there a magic formula for success? Maybe. Success leaves clues. To be successful, you must do what successful people do! If you want to be rich, you must only own some prime real estate or own equity in a up-and-coming company.

Wealthy people have known this for years! If you want to be a successful marketer, you can do the following things:

1. Use the moves I teach in this book.
2. Develop your own moves.
3. Copy someone else.

Let's discuss all three. First, use the moves I teach in this book. These moves are time-tested, proven, and used by top-notch marketing professionals across the world. Simply apply a few moves, and you will immediately see a dramatic change in your marketing effectiveness. You can then fine-tune and modify these movies for your particular business.

Alternatively, you can go out and develop new ways to generate sales revenue. More than likely, through trial and error, you may find something. Or you can study your competitors and copy what they do.

Guess which is the easiest? Take the proven strategy and make it better. I am always looking around in business to see what is working. If I see a marketing strategy or move that generates revenue, I immediately interview the business owner for details. Then I try to improve it, adapt it, and apply it to my business. It's far easier to work with a proven strategy than it is to start from scratch. If you study any new business idea or breakthrough, you will find it is not truly new—it's 10 percent better than the way someone else did it.

Most people think they need to work alone in marketing. Black belt marketers don't agree with this; they like to take what works for other people and build on it. If you do exactly the same thing someone else does, you will get the same results. If others have already figured it out, take advantage of it! People have made millions of dollars in direct marketing by renting lists of well-qualified prospects and mailing powerful value propositions. This is a proven revenue-generating method. Now before you say, "Why would people give you their secrets?" let me tell you another secret that all black belt marketers know.

People will always want to help you if you are sincere and your intentions are noble and good. Tell them you respect what they do and one day you'd like to be like them. Ask them to be your mentor (move 26). All the moves come together to help the black belt marketer succeed.

Repetition, repetition, repetition

MOVE 67

Repetition, repetition, repetition

Studies show that if notes aren't taken people forget 50 percent of a lecture within twenty-four hours, 80 percent in two weeks, and 95 percent within one month. This book is much like a lecture or a course in advanced marketing, but the notes are already taken for you!

This move is not exciting but it is critical.

Repetition is the mother of skill (*Repititio Mater Studiorum Est*).

Practice what I share in this book. Set time aside daily to read, study, and practice these moves until they become habit. As part of your daily routine, you're pulled in many different directions. You'll go back to work and forget that a good product or service is only half the battle. Now you need to show others the value they can gain from it.

Marketing is not a one-time process of running a few ads, sending out a few letters, or making a few sales calls. It is an on-going process of adding value to the lives of others and helping them make informed decisions. Becoming a black belt in marketing takes daily practice. Keep this reference handy, write all over it, highlight sections, and use the moves.

GET YOUR BLACK BELT IN MARKETING

Mind-set is more important than method. Change your perspective through repetition, and using your mind will become a habit for you, a natural way to do business. It's the only way to master the techniques. Use a Post-it note and highlighter, mark some of the moves you work on, and keep going back until these moves become habit.

Reading the book once will give you some great ideas, but if you read it again, you'll get another, and again, another. The secret to learning is space repetition—reviewing the same material over a certain amount of time.

The biggest danger in marketing is to become bored or complacent. Black belt marketers use repetition to keep themselves relevant as the business world changes.

MOVE

68

Command and control

68

Command and control

Most people are indecisive and left to their own accord, are not able to make decisions. This is why education is the best form of marketing. It provides facts, figures, and knowledge to help people make informed decisions. Once you start to educate customers, they will begin to understand your intention is to help them, not take advantage of them. And they will want to help you in return.

When it comes to buying, pulling out money or writing a check most people are indecisive, because they don't want to make a mistake. This is where the black belt marketer comes into action. He gives the customer permission to buy. "It's OK, go ahead and try this product. I promise it will work for you. If it doesn't, just bring it back. You have nothing to lose."

These few simple words inspire confidence and security in the buyer's mind. Today more than ever, buyers are indecisive and confused because they have so many choices and because so many people are trying to get their attention, and there is lack of trust.

Black belt marketers are leaders who want to improve people's lives, not take advantage of them. As such, they command a sales situation. Unless you get people committed to a buying relationship, you cannot build a business. Take away the fear and anxiety people have about starting a business relationship. People are looking to be led, and a black belt marketer will lead for their benefit.

If you truly care for prospects and customers, command with certainty and control the buying process. Reassure your customers and prospects that buying is the right decision. When they use your product and service and find out you've told them the truth, they will love you for leading them to something of value. Never have any doubt about telling your customers what to do, as long as you do it for their best interests.

All leaders command and control. They give clear direction for people to follow. Use of the move of command and control when you see your customers perplexed, confused, or unsure. Give them confidence, and your energy will be transferred.

People are looking for leaders. Black belt marketers lead not follow.

MOVE

69

Outperform anyone's guarantees

MOVE 69

Outperform anyone's guarantees

As you already know, the biggest obstacle that keeps people from buying is trust (move 4). This is no reflection on you, but a sad reflection on the state of marketing today. There are too many marketers out there who are out to make a quick buck. As a black belt marketer, you understand that business is not simply a transactional process but a relationship: a long-lasting relationship process.

The only way to build trust is to deliver beyond what you promise. Certainly, offering a great product that delivers is wonderful, and having a guarantee to back up your claims makes it easier for customers to make a purchase decision. But having a guarantee that makes it almost impossible not to try or buy is what will make an unbelievable difference. Herein lies another black belt marketing secret: The longer the money-back guarantee, the more likely people are to try it and the less likely they are to return it. People want protection of their purchase in the form of a guarantee, but few will actually use it.

Black belt marketers protect their buyers by assuming the risk of the purchase. If people can try your product and know with certainty they can return it, buying becomes a much easier decision.

GET YOUR BLACK BELT IN MARKETING

Black belt marketers understand what people want and the factors that influence the customers' decision before the sell. The market tests integrity.

Would you buy a CD series from someone who gives a one-year guarantee or a three-month guarantee? We both know the answer to that. Remember a fundamental truth of marketing: people will gravitate to where they can gain maximum value. Adding extended warranties and guarantees does not cost much more, and the benefits far exceed the costs.

Notice how these moves build on each other. Whatever the nature of your product or service, try doubling the length of the money-back guarantee and notice what happens. The increase in sales volume will far outstrip the returns.

Black belt marketers think in reverse of conventional marketers. They have no fears because they know they bring true value to the marketplace and deliver the results that people expect.

This is a simple but powerful move. Take advantage of it!

70

Know that empathy sells

MOVE 70

Know that empathy sells

I n move number five, we talked about walking in your customers' shoes. This was about understanding what your market and customers value from a product-solution viewpoint. But as a black belt marketer, you know that you are dealing with human beings, and as such you need to understand how they buy. All buyers want to be heard and understood, and this means that you have to master a skill called empathy, which is the ability to understand and relate to others at a psychological level.

Some people call the ability to connect with anyone at anytime and in any place, people skills. To connect with prospects, suspects, customers, and employees you need only do one thing: be empathetic.

Empathy, as quoted in Webster's English Dictionary, is "One's ability to recognize, perceive, and directly experientially feel the emotion of another."

Empathy respects the feelings of others. Whatever the nature of your business, you deal with people all the time. If you want to connect with them, you must have care and consideration for their feelings.

Empathy comes through great listening skills, not just through asking questions. People want to be heard. I have a friend who knows a prime minister, and he occasionally wines and dines dignitaries with him. The friend explains to me that within minutes, the prime minister can make another person feel at ease and like the most important person on the planet. It's an invaluable skill. How does he do this? By showing empathy

1. Provide the speaker with your undivided attention, and make direct eye contact.

2. However trivial the issue, do not be judgmental. Listen and acknowledge that you truly understand the problem and can relate to it—even if it's not the first time you have heard about the issue.

3. Observe the emotions behind the words. Is the speaker angry, afraid, frustrated, or resentful? Respond to and validate the emotion as well as the words.

4. Be quiet. Don't feel you must have an immediate reply. Often, if you allow for a lapse after the speaker has vented, they will break the silence and offer a solution.

5. Assure your understanding. Ask clarifying questions and restate what you perceive the speaker to be saying.

People want to be heard. Your job as a black belt marketer is to be a counselor with great listening skills. People love to talk about themselves! You can't go wrong if you find out what is of value to them.

What does a best friend do for you? She listens and gives great advice. If you truly care about your customers, their success, their dreams and desires, you will want to listen to them.

Black belt marketers know that once you help your customers and prospects and are empathetic, they will by default want to help you.

71

Surprise your customers

MOVE 71

Surprise your customers

Black belt marketers know marketing is a lifetime process, not a single event. You must continually keep excitement in the process by aiming to surprise your customers.

Continually keep the customer informed, educated, involved, and entertained.

One of the best things to do is to give surprise gifts as a thank-you for being a loyal customer. Your marketing budget will stretch a lot farther on people who already have a relationship with you than those who do not. Although you may already see your customers as dear friends or client, giving a gift shows them you are thinking about them.

Gifts are one of the best ways to build relationships and to show people you love them. Didn't you do it when you were dating?

Continue to build trust by giving gifts out of the goodness of your heart and for no other reason than to show appreciation. You may call it customer appreciation, but it's really just good business practice.

GET YOUR BLACK BELT IN MARKETING

A golden rule of sales: If you think about your customers, they will think of you. When you make people feel special, they will make you feel special.

Do the unexpected, and people will talk about you. A company I consult for in Silicon Valley, California, is planning to hold its next user-group meeting at a beautiful Mexican resort. The CEO took my advice seriously: Surprise people!

This is an intangible aspect of value, and the market always gravitates to where it can gain the most perceived value. Any company with a strong brand does extraordinary things for its customers. American Express is a good example by sending gift certificates and rewards to their most loyal customers. Surprised customers won't forget the favor. It's a major reason for Amex's success.

Customer appreciation days, lunches and dinners are great gifts! My local dentist is one of the most successful children's orthodontists in the area. He offers free movie tickets occasionally, and the kids talk about him at school!

Go through your database, and plan something special for your customers. Everyone loves a surprise gift!

MOVE

72

Be disciplined and systematic in your sales efforts

72

Be disciplined and systematic in your sales efforts

We've hammered through numerous marketing moves and strategies. Now let's talk about how the moves all come together and how important it is to go about your sales process in a systematic fashion.

Have you ever wondered why franchises are so successful? They follow a defined system and have policies and procedures for everything. Last week's complaints become next week's to-do list, and soon become part of the operating procedure. This may be part of the reason that franchises have close to a 90 percent success ratio.

Black belt marketing does not happen by chance; black belt marketing is a result of a well-thought-out plan that accomplishes the following:

1. Attracts suspects (those who may be interested in purchasing)

2. Converts suspects to well-qualified prospects (those with the money and a strong desire to buy)

3. Converts prospects into paying customers

4. Gets customers to provide referrals

GET YOUR BLACK BELT IN MARKETING

Black belt marketing is a defined path for closing the sale. Let's walk through it.

A. GETTING SUSPECTS

Your competition hopes that suspects will simply show up. But a black belt marketer understands he is in control of the lead-generation process. There are a number of ways to generate leads, but one of the best is to provide valuable *free* reports, samples, and materials. Build trust!

Successful marketers have a constant stream of leads coming in. You will know your lead-generation program is working when people are always inquiring about your product or service.

B. CONVERT SUSPECTS TO PROSPECTS

All suspects should be qualified. Not everyone who inquires will have the money or will decide to make a purchase immediately. Top sales people focus on well-qualified leads. Quickly qualify leads by using a questionnaire or other filters. Then make appointments either in person or over the phone.

C. CLOSE WELL-QUALIFIED PROSPECTS

The way to convert a well-qualified prospect into a customer is by showing the immense value they are likely to gain in using your product or service. Handle any objections openly and truly add value. Some ways you can add value are by giving a quality presentation or allowing your customers to try your product or service risk-free, with no strings or obligations.

D. GET REFERRALS FROM CUSTOMERS

Use referrals to get more qualified prospects as quickly as possible. Referrals are the quickest way to acquire more qualified prospects instead of suspects. People who are referred are more likely to buy because they have gone through the trust-building factor.

This is the complete sales cycle in action. If sales are down, identify which step is missing. That's the beauty of the system. Ensure you have a system for whatever marketing activity you do. By definition, a system is something that produces repeatable and predictable results.

Turn life into a marketing university

73

Turn life into a marketing university

Black belt marketers observe what's happening around them. How are people marketing? As you drive to work, go on a walk, or sit in an airport lounge, notice the words marketers use to get your attention. Visit newsstands and look at signs. If these messages attract you, they will also attract others.

Many of the best marketing ideas come from other people. Your customers will give you great ideas, because these are the people you ultimately aim to satisfy. The best marketers are curious, always wanting to learn more, always observing, and always asking questions. Here's how to get started in turning your life into a marketing university:

1. AS OF TODAY, DON'T THROW JUNK MAIL AWAY WITHOUT STUDYING IT.

Take five minutes each day to look at junk mail. Somebody took a lot of time, effort, and money to send it to you. Which pieces appeal to you? Why? What words and phrases get your attention? Can you use any of them for your marketing campaign? Don't try to reinvent, simply adapt and adopt what works. Keep the pieces that make you want to take action. If you feel this way, others will too. Call the person who sent the best junk mail and tell them how impressed you are. Tell them you'd

403

like to do something similar for your business. Ask them how much it costs, and could you talk with someone in the marketing department?

2. STUDY HEADLINES AT NEWSSTANDS.

Next time you are in line at the grocery store, look at the *National Inquirer, BusinessWeek, Newsweek,* and others. Look at the headlines. Do they get your attention? Why? Could you adapt these headlines to meet your needs?

3. ORDER AND TRY COMPETITIVE PRODUCTS.

Act as a customer and you will gain real customer experience. Rank the competition:

- How do they sell?

- How do they handle the order?

- How do they deliver the product or service?

- Did they over-promise and under-deliver?

- What key words and phrases do they use to sell?

- How is their after-sale support?

- How are they different from and/or better than your product or service?

Study the competitions' Web site. Remember, success leaves clues. Successful companies have tested and found something that works well. Write out a list of things you can improve based on the survey. Then develop an action plan to do it.

4. INTERVIEW THE MANAGERS OF SUCCESSFUL BUSINESSES.

What works in another business can often be applied to yours. When you go about your daily affairs and see a business that appears to be doing well, call and ask to interview the owner or manager. Be honest and tell them you are impressed with their marketing and would like to learn more. In return, offer lunch or dinner. Most people will be more than happy to share their ideas with you if you are not a competitor. This is how I have learned many of my moves!

5. GET X-RAY VISION.

Black belt marketers see almost everything as an opportunity. Other people aren't trained to recognize opportunity. You, however, look at everything going on around you. Can you:

- Partner with someone?
- Mirror what they do?
- Adapt and adopt what they do?

Black belts see marketing as a real-time university. When you see a new product or idea, remember that someone has solved a new problem through careful observation. Whatever you want to do, someone is doing it right now in front of your eyes.

Black belt marketers are not made but are nurtured through careful observation and study.

MOVE

74

Know the best form of
marketing is the truth

74

Know the best form of marketing is the truth

The real challenge faced by black belt marketers is the test of integrity. Most marketers get seduced into making promises they cannot deliver. You can sell *any* product if you tell people it will solve all their problems.

But never fall into this trap! Do not only point out the value of your product or service; always be honest about its shortcomings. Your prospects will respect you for it. It shows them that you have done your homework and are well aware of the options and alternatives available.

If you feel your product or service does not fit the requirements of your prospect, it is your obligation as a black belt marketer to say so. Otherwise, you do your prospect and yourself an injustice. Over time your prospect will learn the truth, and you will have destroyed your reputation and credibility.

THE TRUTH SELLS!
Not everyone will become your customer. Focus on those you can add the most value to. Many marketing books teach market segmentation; a good one would be *Marketing Management* by Phil Kotler. Segmen-

GET YOUR BLACK BELT IN MARKETING

tation is the process of identifying prospects that you can add the most value to. It's human nature to say, "What's the catch?" What if you tell them upfront why you are making the offer? What if I said, "I prepared five thousand CDs for a seminar that was cancelled. I don't intend to do another seminar for six months. I'll use the money from this sale to produce another audio series. So I'm offering these CDs at 50 percent off!"

It's not only more appealing, it's the truth.

Every marketing activity you do tests and builds integrity. Tell the truth in all your marketing communications. It will set you apart. People respect the truth and can read your sincerity. Business is about serving others. To be a marketing master, be a person of the highest ethical standards.

Your goal is not to outsmart customers but to outsmart the competition by focusing on the customer! Do this by being truthful. Let the competition do the hype; it will surely catch up with them.

How about writing to existing customers or posting a sign that says, "As a small business, we do not have a Madison Avenue advertising budget. To keep our costs down to you, we grow our business based on referrals. Give us referrals, and we'll be able to grow and bring you better products. Please let your friends know of the great work we do. Thank you!"

The black belt marketer understands and respects the power of the truth.

MOVE

75

Never stop marketing

MOVE 75

Never stop marketing

You already know there is a direct relationship between sales and marketing. Sales go down, because marketing is going down too. People no longer see value in what you have to offer. Black belt marketers know people have short memories. If you don't continuously remind them of the value you bring to them, someone else will.

Whatever mechanism you choose to show the market the value to be gained, be consistent. Define a budget for the year. One or two ads or five mailings will not make customers show up. Successful and well-known businesses become that way through the consistency of their marketing. They have created a brand in the marketplace (move 80).

If sales go up and down, it means the marketing is also inconsistent. Sales usually occur several weeks or months after a marketing or value campaign. To ensure constant sales, the marketing campaign must also be consistent. It's a huge mistake to stop marketing if sales are down. The delay in seeing results from marketing can be days, weeks, months—even years. Never stop marketing. Never stop showing people how you can add value to their lives.

GET YOUR BLACK BELT IN MARKETING

Marketing is not something you do once. It is not a transactional process but a perpetual process. Focus on educating your market on a regular basis. Send out mailings, do conference calls, visit, and send gifts. Consistent marketing builds trust, and trust is the number one reason people buy from you. A car will stop if you don't give it fuel, and sales will stop unless you continue to show the market you can add value.

Never get complacent about marketing. When marketing stops, so does business.

MOVE
76

Make the most of your Web site

76

Make the most of your Web site

Most of the Web sites that you see today are simply static bro-
chures, and most Web sites are designed without a purpose. As
a black belt marketer, your Web site is focused on generating
leads—people you want to build a long-term relationship with that will
eventually buy product and refer you to others. Irrespective of the size
of your business, you need a Web site. This shows people that you are a
true professional and are committed to your business.

A Web site is simply your virtual office or place of business. It is an exten-
sion of your brick-and-mortar business. You need to treat visitors the same
online as you would if they visited your physical location. We will shortly
be talking about how to lay out your Web site and make it functional.

What most marketers forget is that the person visiting the site is a
human being, not a computer, and they need to be treated as such. As a
black belt marketer, you are trained in understanding human behavior.
The person that visits your Web site is here for a reason, just as if they
came to your physical office, and you need to ask them, "Why are you
here? How can I help you?"

It was not by luck or chance that they arrived; they had a purpose for selecting the keyword that brought them to your site. They are looking to satisfy an itch. Your job is to find out what the itch is. The only problem is that you have less than a few seconds to do so. This is why all black belt marketers' Web sites will have an introductory video welcoming the person and asking them to leave their name and details so that the marketer can follow up and get details on the itch!

It is estimated that 90 percent of all visitors to Web sites usually leave without making any purchase. The Web is a place where people browse, not dissimilar to window shopping. So how do we make money with our Web site? This is done by knowing the Web revenue-generating formula, which is only known to black belt marketers.

Web Revenue = Visitors x Conversion Ratio x Average Transaction Size x Frequency

To make money on the Web, you only need to do three things:

- Get people to visit your Web site
- Convert these visitors into paying customers
- Get them to come back often and refer others

And there are proven strategies to achieve each of the above, which we will be discussing shortly. But the most important thing that you know as a black belt marketer is that the only real difference between online marketing and offline marketing is that in the case of the Web, the person that is visiting your place of business is a qualified prospect—they found you, they typed in a keyword, and they are interested in what you have to offer. So your success now boils down to your ability to close them. You are, for the most part, not dealing with tire kickers, but well-qualified prospects. The Web has done most of the dirty work for you. There are lukewarm leads.

The biggest mistake marketers make is assuming that visitors to their site will immediately become buyers. As I pointed out in move number two, people only buy from sellers that they know, like, and trust, be that a person or a brand. So your goal as a black belt marketer is to build

418

trust as quickly as possible; once you have their details and to develop a relationship with them. How do you do this? By offering them something in return for their personal details.

Most black belt marketers offer a free report of some kind, something that the visitor may be interested in receiving and reviewing, in return for visitors providing their contact details.

A name and e-mail address captured online is the same as getting a business card offline. And as a black belt marketer, you know that it could be several months before this name and e-mail address will turn into an order. You now need to follow up with a progressive educational program showing the prospects incremental value and providing a reason why they should purchase from you and why you are best suited to solve their problem.

Most marketers do not have the stamina to follow up and follow through with leads, be that online or offline. But as a black belt marketer, you know that all the wealth in marketing is on the back end.

Most traditional marketers are also obsessed with getting traffic, and little thought is given to how to convert traffic or visitors into dollars. This goes back to conventional offline marketing.

Traffic---------Relationship---------Trust---------Sale

There are no shortcuts in marketing. Just like a good recipe, you need to follow it step-by-step. In online marketing, it is highly unlikely that people will visit your Web site and buy from it unless they know you, like you, and trust you or your brand. A true black belt marketer will use the Web for lead generation, then do a master move, which is build a relationship with prospects, and they do this by "getting them offline as soon as possible." The only way to build a true and lasting relationship with someone is to meet them in person or at least talk with them.

GET YOUR BLACK BELT IN MARKETING

As such a black belt marketer will set up a direct-mailing program or set up a teleconference call with all the leads that have been captured on the Web. This usually would be over a period of a few weeks. The black belt marketer knows that they are dealing with a prospect; this person has an itch, has a need, and is looking for a solution. They simply need to be qualified and subsequently closed. And education is the best way to close a sale.

The biggest problem with Web sites today is that the people that put them up assume that a Web site can solve all of their problems. They have technical support, product information, e-commerce, company information, investor information, and the like. This all becomes overwhelming and confusing to visitors. A black belt marketer knows that the more relevant the message is to your audience, the more likely it is that they will want to leave their details to learn more.

Ideally, you want to set up a separate landing page for each product or service that you offer.

Now that we understand a little about the Web and how black belt marketers leverage the Web, let's look at how black belt marketers set up their Web sites.

1. MAKE SURE YOUR SITE IS FUNCTIONAL.

A Web page is simply a series of pages. The only difference is that these pages are now online. But a Web page is different to a conventional direct marketing page because people have chosen to read this page, compared to you sending it to them unsolicited.

The secret to a functional Web site is that it should be viewed as if someone were walking into your store. How would you treat someone that came to your office or place of business to learn about what you do? What would you say? What would you show them, assuming they know very little about what you do?

Keys to a good Web site are:
- Quick access to needed information. Give visitors information instead of just telling them how great you are. The more free information you offer, the more they will respect you and the more often they will want to visit your site.

- Ease of navigation. Can a visitor get to needed pages without too many clicks?

- Good copy. Headlines get attention. The same copy skills apply to the Web. If people read the first fifty words, they will read the rest.

- Constant testing. There is no final or perfect site. Change things around and see how it affects traffic.

- A good database. Provide a place on the site to capture names and e-mails. The whole of Web marketing revolves around having a database.

2. ENSURE A PROFESSIONAL IMAGE.

To build trust at your site, consider the following:
- Let visitors know you will not share information (privacy policy).

- Use recognizable credit card logos if you sell online.

- Become a member of the BBB (Better Business Bureau), a well-respected name that adds credibility.

- Use testimonials to build credibility immediately.

- Offer samples or free offers.

3. GET TRAFFIC.

There are basically two ways to get traffic to your Web site that all black belt marketers know. They are:

1. Unpaid/Organic
2. Paid

Organic traffic will visit your Web site as a result of a keyword search. Or you have an affiliate relationship with another site. But in both cases, you are not paying for the traffic. The other way is to run advertisements that get people to visit your site, such as Google ad words or banner ads.

Both of these strategies, can be broken down into the following three sub categories

Buy   Paid
Build   Organic
Borrow   Organic

BUY/PAID

You can either do banner advertising or run conventional Web advertising to buy traffic. It's expensive and similar to running conventional newspaper ads. One of the best ways to get traffic to your site is to use Google Ads. This is called pay-per-click advertising. You only pay for the people that actually visit your site. The guru of Google Ads is Perry Marshall, who wrote Ultimate guide to Google Adwords. I highly recommend that you read this book.

BUILD/ORGANIC

The secret to the web can be summarized in one word: content. Search engines will pick up your Web site based on its content. Black belt marketers know that the Web rewards content. The more articles you submit via PRWeb or newsletters, the more chance of you ranking high on the search engines.

The more you write and submit to the Web, the higher your ranking will be and the more traffic you will have. You can build traffic to your

site by posting reports and press releases to the site. Black belt marketers know the more new information posted to the Web site, the more
likely it is for your name to be picked up by a search engine. The Web
rewards those people who contribute the most content. It's also a great
way to differentiate you from an estimated fifty million active sites. The
Web is just another database, and the more you post to the database, the
more likely you will be picked up. Internet gurus call this strategy the
SEO strategy, or search engine optimization strategy. A strategy used to
insure that search engines find you, before anyone else.

BORROW/ORGANIC

Joint ventures and strategic alliances are a big part of Web marketing.
Have someone endorse you or send traffic your way via a link. It bor-
rows on other's traffic.

Building and borrowing are powerful and cost-effective options. The black
belt marketer focuses his or her energy here.

Mastering the Web is a book in itself, and it is an evolving technology. As
a black belt marketer, understanding and mastering the Web is an important part of your marketing strategy.

MOVE
77

Be or get a spokesperson

77

Be or get a spokesperson

Remember, products sell because of the trust factor. People buy because they see some value in your product or service. You become someone they trust to deliver the desired value better than anyone else (move four). How do you do this?

One way to establish trust with potential customers is by becoming a spokesperson or hiring a respected celebrity. Most successful products have a spokesperson behind them. The most successful car dealers in the United States have an owner or manager become the spokesperson.

As a customer, if I see you, I believe you and start to trust you.

Kentucky Fried Chicken and Colonel Sanders lived on long after the colonel passed away, because the Colonel developed a loyal following. His image is still the major selling point for KFC.

Can you hire celebrities? Yes, celebrities can be hired from Hollywood movie brokers (find these brokers on the Internet). They will contact the celebrity and work out a deal. You won't even need the celebrity for long, just for shooting a video. Another option is to hire a leader in your field to become your spokesperson.

If you truly have a consumer-focused product or service and you get someone famous behind it, you'll hit a home run. Having a spokesperson is similar to getting a testimonial. Third-party or independent validation counts heavily in the world of marketing.

Notice how most infomercials use famous actors because people buy based on trust. They trust the spokesperson will not mislead them. The spokesperson is a hero, a person of integrity. I hear you saying, "I could never afford that!" It's not as hard as you may think. Many celebrities (even local ones) could gain substantial benefit from your product. If they do, they may be more than willing to act as a spokesperson, especially if they use your product or service and see benefit in it. Having a famous celebrity refer to your product is identical to getting referrals. Because the referrer is well-known, the impact can be powerful.

Structure whatever type of deal you want: a fixed payment or a percentage of royalties. If you don't have the budget to hire a celebrity, be your own spokesperson. One example of this is Men's Wearhouse founder George Zimmer: "You're going to like the way you look. I guarantee it." He owns 8.7 percent of Men's Wearhouse, a stake worth an estimated $94 million in 2004, as quoted on Yahoo!, and he's the spokesperson for his own company.

Even a small business owner can use this tactic. For example, a repair person could develop and appear in his own video for less than two thousand dollars. Say something like: "You have my word; you will be satisfied with the work I do, or you don't pay me."

Run the video for ten dollars per spot on cable (move seventeen), and reach several hundred thousand people. Your phone won't stop ringing because people will see you and begin to trust you. It works! You don't have to be filthy rich to be on television or to hire a celebrity. You just need to know how to do it!

MOVE

78

Give more than you
expect to receive

MOVE 78

Give more than you expect to receive

Black belt marketing is about making people's lives better and bringing them the value they want and expect. Most of all, it's fun, because you have the opportunity to improve the quality of your customers' lives. Black belt marketers become wealthy in the process, not because they seek wealth but because they seek to help others. It's a unique mind-set.

I must give first; then I will receive.

As you earn your black belt in marketing and we approach the end of our training, here's a recap: Never ever sell, just help people buy. No one wants to be sold, but everyone loves to buy. People want you to make it easy for them to make informed and intelligent decisions. At the same time, they want to feel in control of the purchase. That's why education is the best way to sell. You simply provide facts, figures, and success stories/testimonials. It gives people a comfort level and makes them feel they're making the right decision by buying your product or service.

Referrals work beautifully. People trust those who refer them because their recommendation is based on experience.

GET YOUR BLACK BELT IN MARKETING

Black belt marketers know that marketing is about getting people to make purchase decisions, and the best way to do it is to provide facts, figures, and testimonials that support the case.

Once people see the significance of what you offer to their lives and businesses, they will surely buy from you. As part of your marketing, aim to give your prospects more facts, information, samples, trials, and guarantees than anyone else. This not only allows them to make a decision more quickly but allows you to build credibility and trust rapidly.

Your job as a black belt marketer is to help people see the value, because it's not always obvious. Once they see the value, they will be in a position to make an informed decision. Your mind-set is to provide more value than any other marketer does. Black belt marketers remain externally focused:

If you help people, they will want to help you. It is a universal law. Your obsession should be to improve the lives of others by giving them what they want; then they'll want to help you in return. The more you give, the more you get back. Trust me.

I spend a lot of time on the phone giving people marketing advice, and they benefit from my knowledge so they automatically want to help me in return. I don't even need to ask for the help; they simply volunteer it.

People will not invest in you unless you invest in them first. Get people to understand that you're the real thing by sending out free reports and samples. When you do, your world will change. Black belt marketers provide so much more value than anyone else because they have the mind-set of serving others.

I once gave sales training to a sales representative at a television station. We spent an hour on the phone once a week for two months. I had no idea what I would get at the end of it. I just wanted her to benefit from my knowledge. She was able to market so much more effectively that she invited me to appear on a TV show to introduce me to her friends in the media world. She is now one of my biggest fans! It happened simply because I focused on helping her succeed at her job!

Focus on your customers' success, and your success is always guaranteed.

When your customers are successful, you cannot not help but be successful. Money is simply the reward for helping others. Most of your competition has its own self-interest at heart, and this makes it easy for you! Your sincerity and honesty is automatically transmitted to others when you talk to a prospect or customer and you feel in your heart that you want to help them. You see them as valued friends and family members (move 3), and they respond to you. If you simply want to make money, your customers will sense it and move away.

It makes no difference how many marketing books you study, unless you know that you become successful by putting others' success ahead of your own. When people gain value from your knowledge, they're eager to help you. Black belt marketers know this only happens when you give more than you ever expect to receive.

MOVE
79

The more you tell,
the more you sell

79

The more you tell, the more you sell

Black belt marketers know a secret that conventional marketers do not: The more you tell, the more you sell.

The longer your advertisement, the longer your letter, the longer your sales call, the longer your radio or TV ad, the more likely you are to gain a prospect's interest and lead them to take action by buying your product or service. If you study all the marketing gurus—such as Jay Abraham , Jay Conrad Levinson, and Claude Hopkins—they all agree that long copy sells! As your copy is simply "salesmanship in print."

You may not think people read long letters, but this is not true. A book is a long letter, and you will read it from cover to cover if it has information that will enhance your life. There are certainly people who don't like to read. Perhaps they prefer to listen, but even then they listen to the complete message.

Black belt marketers know relevant, pertinent letters will be read by their prospects. But it's tough to write a long letter and keep the reader engaged—only world-class copywriters can write a several-page letter and keep the reader engaged until the last page. It helps to view a sales letter just like a salesperson standing in front of you. What do you expect from this person? You'd prefer as much quality information and education as possible. A sales letter is no more than salesmanship in print.

This is the reverse of what most conventional marketers think. And the danger is they provide their prospects with too little information. People are hungry for the information you have to offer: information will help them make an informed decision.

Your goal is to provide so much value in the form of high-quality and relevant information. It can be printed matter, videos, CDs, samples, anything. Because customers trust you to solve problems, let them know you are not hiding anything and that you want to help by answering all objections.

In my early days, I sold to Procter & Gamble, the world-famous consumer products company. To win the sale, we showed them exactly how we made the product. We invited them to our manufacturing plant, and they even knew how much money we made. But all of this benefited us, because the more we told the more we sold!

After reading your sales letter or e-mail, a prospect should feel satisfied that every possible objection, issue, and concern has been met. The prospect should feel you are the only viable solution to their problem.

This is one of the harder moves to master, because no one has taught us how to write long letters, e-mails, and advertisements.

When I give a presentation, I tell people how hard I work at marketing—all the books I've read, the tapes I've listened to, the conferences I've attended. It shows my commitment to the field and increases my perceived value in the eyes of the audience. They feel they learn useful information and want to be associated with me. The more I tell, the more I sell!

MOVE
80

Get the ultimate reward:
A brand

80

Get the ultimate reward: A brand

The result of black belt marketing is the creation of your brand. People will know your promise, who you are, what you do, and a get a positive feeling when they think about you. The ultimate reward for the products and services of black belt marketers is to become a well-respected brand.

A brand is a promise, the feeling of comfort and security that people get when they think of your product or service. However small your business may be, you already have a brand image—the way people currently think about you and how you deliver on your promises.

An estimated 50 to 80 percent of the valuation of a consumer brand company is based on its brand portfolio or names, but these are simply names, nothing else. They are not tangible. Some of the most famous brands in the world are household names, and billions are spent in building these names and logos over the years. There is immense power in a name and a logo! Here are the world's top ten brands, taken from a *BusinessWeek* survey from May 2004, in order of name recognition:

GET YOUR BLACK BELT IN MARKETING

Coca-Cola
Microsoft
IBM
GE
Intel
Nokia
Toyota
Disney
McDonald's
Mercedes-Benz

If you want a soft drink, who do you think of? If you need software, where do you go? If you want a computer, who's considered the best? Your answers are based on branding, the level of trust and comfort you feel when the name appears. Your brand ultimately equates to how much money you make in the long-term, and black belt marketers do whatever they can to fight aggressively to protect their brand name.

Great brands are created over decades, through consistency. Here are the four steps to creating a brand.

1. CREATE A POSITIONING FIRST.

The starting point to create a brand is to create the positioning. Positioning is how you want the market to see you. Black belt marketers decide how they want to be seen in the marketplace. They are proactive, not reactive, and create a vision for how the world should see them. The market does not create the brand; the people behind the brand create the position of the brand in the market.

Positioning is the general direction in which you move. You determine the future for your product or service and how you want the world to view it! Where do you see yourself in the market? Or better still, how do you want to be seen in the market?

442

Positioning is your guide to where you are headed. It is your direction. Others arrive at the same destination through your vision and messaging.

Share your position with those who promote your business. To help you understand how it works, I'll share with you my positioning. "I believe marketing is broad and multidimensional and can be used by anyone at any stage of life—be it a student, doctor, housewife, or business professional. It is a set of tools used to bring perceived value to the marketplace. I am unique because I see the world in color, whereas most marketing experts see it in black and white (for business only). My passion is to help people use marketing to improve their lives."

This is what I say to anyone doing publicity for me.

2. DEVELOP A TAG LINE.

A tag line falls out of your positioning. It is a simple one-liner. Mine is "Marketing is for everybody, including you!"
Notice how I condensed my positioning into a simple one-liner that brings it all together. A world-class advertising agency could charge hundreds of thousands of dollars to come up with a tag line. Once your tag line gets into the minds of the masses, it either attracts them or moves them away from you. People are attracted by what you say and the significance of your words to their lives.

3. START THE MESSAGING.

The messaging falls under both the positioning and tag line and supports both. The messaging includes the supporting points of your positioning. Everything I say falls under the concept of seeing marketing as multidimensional. I always refer back to the fact that marketing is for everybody. Although I may talk about marketing for college students, dentists, job hunters, or business people, I always keep in mind its universality.

4. CREATE YOUR BRAND.

A brand is simply a message communicated over time to create a personality. When you think of that brand, it gives you an emotional feeling. Branding is about creating a promise and personality. (Again the Ps of marketing in action.)

There is no real person named IBM, Microsoft, or Coca-Cola. You prefer to see them as a personality, because the names give you comfort, security, and confidence. Branding takes advantage of psychology: All humans need a sense of security. A trusted brand gives us that security through its promise.

It's important for black belt marketers to know about consistency in branding.

A brand is created when people identify your name or logo with a particular result. For instance, Honda is a well-respected brand, but more than their name sets them apart. The exact typeset of the name also makes a difference.

The font style of the trademark and the size of the Honda logo have been the same since Soichiro Honda founded the company in 1948. The Honda marketing department, in fact, has a manual on how the Honda name should be written. It must be written in this way every time it is displayed.

A brand is created through consistent messaging. In black belt marketing, consistency is key. That consistency is built in the way your name or logo appears in public and the result people get from using your product or service.

MOVE 80: GET THE ULTIMATE REWARD - A BRAND

You may think of Microsoft as a four-hundred-pound gorilla! Yet Microsoft is simply a name. The image created is really a powerful illusion. Branding is not limited to large multinational organizations; you're a brand, your product is a brand, and you will only achieve success to the extent that people recognize and respect the brand.

The end game of marketing is about what your product or service becomes in the eyes of your customer. The way it's measured is through branding.

Most of your competition will never develop a brand, because they won't take the time to create consistent messaging. But black belt marketers know better.

MOVE
81

Execute black belt style

MOVE 81

Execute black belt style

Confidence and competence comes not through listening but through doing. The final move to master in order to get your black belt is the ability to focus (Follow One Course Until Successful). There are many daily distractions in any business. But as a black belt marketer, you are a *master of focus.*

The most important time is time you give yourself. Focus on a few moves and practice them daily. Don't do these moves just once—make them a part of the natural way you do business, starting today. Do not be content with simply using a few moves. Do a wide array of them repeatedly on a daily basis. For example, continue to ask for referrals and don't just settle for asking once. Ask repeatedly.

Never get complacent; Keep this book handy, as it is meant to be a reference guide. Review it regularly as your roadmap and blueprint for business growth.

A true black belt has flawless execution skills. This means you know what to do and do it. Don't make a U-turn once the commitment is made. Your competition may be inspired for the moment by reading some of the moves in this book, and then a few hours later go back to doing things the same old way. See an opportunity to add value and seize it. You are a person of tremendous character.

I have written two books and thirty reports on marketing because I see the opportunity to add value in different areas of life to market effectively. I was distracted at times and could have given up, but I followed through and made it happen.

I am no smarter than anyone else. I just care about helping others benefit from the power that marketing offers.

The ability to follow through is a key characteristic of black belts. They say what they do and do what they say. You will stand out with your ability to implement the revenue-generating strategies we've discussed. Strengthen your marketing muscle by repeatedly practicing these moves.

Many times, people get excited when they learn new information, but, just like an exponential curve, it dies down over the next thirty days. The key to your success now is to have a thirty-, sixty-, and ninety-day plan to implement the proven marketing moves in this book.

Daily practice creates a habit, and a habit soon becomes a way of life. Gain momentum by trying a move, getting a result, and building on it. You know it works, and there is nothing like success to build success.

You may have heard the saying that there are only three types of people:

1.   Those who make things happen
2.   Those who watch what happened
3.   Those who have no idea what happened

Black belts are number one. They don't wait for things to happen; they make them happen. You have at your disposal the strategies to make an immediate change in your business, so keep this handbook in close reach. Focus is the key to your success! Psychologists know the mind is incredibly powerful, and, when focused, it will work to perfection. Yet the mind loves to wander, and it can easily get distracted. It needs to be managed!

Jim Rohn, America's foremost business philosopher, said, "No one can do push-ups for you; you must do them yourself."

You have in your hands one of the most powerful books on marketing. Only when you can generate sales are you a true businessperson, and the knowledge in this book shows you how to do it.

Do the work, continue to train, make it a habit to read this book several times until the moves become a habit for you.

The best compliment you can pay masters is to surpass them. You have the ability to be a MGM (Marketing Grand Master) and to teach others. I hope that long after I am gone, there will be many MGMs to help others market effectively and add value to others' lives and contribute to our planet.

Thank you for allowing me to be your coach!

With respect,

Ali Pervez

ABOUT THE AUTHOR

Ali Pervez is one of America's leading marketing experts who pas-
sionately believes that marketing is
for everyone. His work focuses on
helping not only organizations, but
also individuals in improving their
effectiveness in marketing.

He is the author of the book *Marketing is King!*, has over 20 years
of global marketing experience, and
has done marketing projects in 22
countries outside of the U.S. Starting
as a marketing analyst, he rose to the
position of Chief Marketing Officer.
He has held senior marketing posi-
tions at start-ups and major U.S. Fortune 500 Companies, including
Abbott Laboratories, Sonoco Products Company, and Robert Half International. At Abbott Laboratories, he was a recipient of two Vice President
Awards for outstanding contribution in marketing within one year. In
four months, he was also able to triple the sales of the division he ran for
one of the fastest growing companies in the U.S., and he nearly tripled the
sales of a Silicon Valley Biotech startup within a year. Mr. Pervez has an
undergraduate degree in Chemistry, Master's degree in Biochemistry, and
also holds an MBA with a distinction project in marketing from the Manchester Business School, U.K. He has been interviewed by the media on
the subject of marketing multiple times, including the BBC. He currently
lives with his wife and two children in the San Francisco Bay area. Learn
more at www.blackbeltinmarketing.com

Your $300 marketing Bonus Gifts!

Thank you for purchasing this book. As a Black Belt Marketer, I always deliver more than you expect. Please go to the link below to download your FREE $300 bonus marketing gifts.

www.blackbeltinmarketing.com/bonusoffer

Respectfully,

Ali Pervez

Take Action & Keep Learning!

Get the full unabridged audio e-book *"Get Your Black Belt in Marketing"*, at a 25% discount! And get my *Ultimate Marketing Guide* <u>Absolutely Free!</u>

If you have read this far, it shows me that you are a true Black Belt Marketer. Statistics show us that we forget 80% of what we learn within two weeks of learning it. To be a true Black Belt Marketer, you must practice the moves in this book daily, until they become a part of your daily marketing routine. I would like to invite you purchase the full unabridged audio e-book of *Get Your Black Belt in Marketing*, for a special discount of 25% off the normal price – just because you have read this book.

Please go to: **www.blackbeltinmarketing.com/audiodownloadoffer** to redeem this special promotion.

In this audio series <u>**you will hear me personally go through all the moves**</u> in this book, in a training format. I will cover all the 81 moves in great detail. The total series is nine hours in length. You will be able to download the moves to your MP3 player immediately, and you will have the Marketing Master with you at all times!

As a special bonus, and my way of saying thank you, I will also give you my *Ultimate Marketing Guide* valued at $99 absolutely FREE! You will be able to learn everything that I learned about Marketing in two decades, in a matter of days. So please take the time to visit the website today to take advantage of these limited time offers, you won't regret it!
Respectfully,

Ali Pervez

BUY A SHARE OF THE FUTURE IN YOUR COMMUNITY

These certificates make great holiday, graduation and birthday gifts that can be personalized with the recipient's name. The cost of one S.H.A.R.E. or one square foot is $54.17. The personalized certificate is suitable for framing and will state the number of shares purchased and the amount of each share, as well as the recipient's name. The home that you participate in "building" will last for many years and will continue to grow in value.

THIS CERTIFIES THAT

YOUR NAME HERE

HAS INVESTED IN A HOME FOR A DESERVING FAMILY

1985-2005

TWENTY YEARS OF BUILDING FUTURES IN OUR COMMUNITY ONE HOME AT A TIME

1200 SQUARE FOOT HOUSE @ $65,000 = $54.17 PER SQUARE FOOT
This certificate represents a tax deductible donation. It has no cash value.

Here is a sample SHARE certificate:

YES, I WOULD LIKE TO HELP!

I support the work that Habitat for Humanity does and I want to be part of the excitement! As a donor, I will receive periodic updates on your construction activities but, more importantly, I know my gift will help a family in our community realize the dream of homeownership. **I would like to SHARE in your efforts against substandard housing in my community!** *(Please print below)*

PLEASE SEND ME _____ SHARES at $54.17 EACH = $ $_____

In Honor Of: _____

Occasion: (Circle One)   HOLIDAY   BIRTHDAY   ANNIVERSARY

OTHER: _____

Address of Recipient: _____

Gift From: _____ *Donor Address:* _____

Donor Email: _____

I AM ENCLOSING A CHECK FOR $ $_____ PAYABLE TO HABITAT FOR HUMANITY <u>OR</u> PLEASE CHARGE MY VISA OR MASTERCARD *(CIRCLE ONE)*

Card Number _____ Expiration Date: _____

Name as it appears on Credit Card _____ Charge Amount $ _____

Signature _____

Billing Address _____

Telephone # Day _____ Eve _____

PLEASE NOTE: Your contribution is tax-deductible to the fullest extent allowed by law.
Habitat for Humanity • P.O. Box 1443 • Newport News, VA 23601 • 757-596-5553
www.HelpHabitatforHumanity.org